101 Creative Dates

Ideas, tips, and personal experiences from

the life of a hopeless romantic

by Matt Taylor

Contents

Introduction

Many of you find it hard to think up new and exciting ideas for dates. I don't blame you. It's not the easiest thing to do, especially in our "Netflix and Chill" kind of world. And no, that does *not* count as a creative date.

People appreciate a bit of creativity now and then, so why not surprise your next date with something different? That's where this book comes in. What will you get out of it? Well, hopefully a whole lot of inspiration, and maybe even a laugh or two at my expense. But seriously, want some cool date ideas that aren't very expensive? I got you covered. Maybe this is your first time going out and you want to make a good impression by doing something different? I got you covered. Are you married and lucky enough to escape the kids for one evening and want to impress your spouse with something different, something unique, and maybe even something magical? Covered. Bored of all the same old date ideas? I. Have. Got. You. Covered.

I was inspired to write this book while lamenting, moping, pouting, over yet another unsuccessful attempt at romance. Let me break it down for you, give you a bit of insight into my dating experience over the past twenty years. While I have great creative date ideas, they don't seem to work for me. And by "work," I mean they haven't led me to The One, yet.

Although I am not a serial dater—despite what some of my good friends might think—girls seem to evade my ingenious attempts to woo them over. Or at least the girls that I'm interested in. *That* is the clincher; finding that mutual interest, that click, that person that you can talk to for hours without getting bored, and when you are done, are left wanting more.

Getting unique with dates was a natural path for me. I've always had creativity in my life, seeing as I come from a family of artists, wood-workers, writers, and more. Also, the imaginative side of me gets to regularly come out through my YouTube cooking channel, *In the Kitchen with Matt*. That one's a lot of fun (and is a great conversation starter). I guess what I'm saying is that all that influence and experience in my life has made me the creative person I am today. The dates in this book are designed for people to have FUN. That's the whole idea, right? Having fun while you get to know someone, and having that fun lead to something more. Since I'm a guy, I'm writing from a man's perspective of planning and executing a date, although I realize that in this day and age, anyone could pull it off. With that in mind, are you ready to change how you see dating? Good. Sit back, relax, and enjoy the ride.

The adventure begins.

Note: All names have been changed to protect the individuals' privacy.

Chapter 1: Cheap Dates

Dollar stretching ideas with full-priced fun

It's not always bad to be a cheapskate. Some of the most rewarding, enjoyable, dates can be ones that don't wind up costing you an arm and a leg. In this section of dates you will find a wide variety of clever ideas that won't break the bank.

Creative Date #1

Elevator Tag: Can you pick the right floor?

What in the world is elevator tag? Well, have you ever seen the movie *Serendipity*? There's a point at the beginning where Kate Beckinsale and John Cusack are in a hotel. I think it was the Waldorf, but it doesn't really matter where they were, it matters what happens there. You see, Kate's character believes in fate, and John just wants to get her phone number because he had the most incredible night of his life with her. Kate says to John as she is in one elevator and John goes to another, "We each pick a button, and if we wind up picking the same floor, then we were meant to be together." If you've seen the movie you know what happens; if you haven't, then watch it—it's a great one.

My inspiration for this date idea came from that movie. This date is designed for at least two people, unless you're really lonely and want to do it by yourself, but that might be a bit odd and would backfire big time. It is really simple and similar to the movie above. You and your date go in one elevator, and another couple goes in the other. Or, you are by yourself and she is by herself. Then each group picks a floor.

Now, there are two scenarios: the elevators can be facing each other, or they can be at each end of the building. If they are facing each other, you just ride the elevator up and down until you hit the same floor the other couple is on. If you happen to be in a building where the elevators are at opposite ends of the building, then you need to walk around a bit on each floor to find your competitors. You can even mix things up and after each floor, and try and switch elevators without getting tagged. Once you're tagged, you're "it," or "out," depending on how you want to play. The thing that matters is having fun and being with your date. Hopefully, said date will watch you pressing elevator buttons like a child and think it's attractive, and totally *not* immature.

What you need for this date:

You will need two different elevators on the same floor in the same building. More than a few floors are best, because then there are more options, with more shiny buttons to press. Elevator Tag can last for quite a while, or it could wind up being short, so you may want to plan something else to go with it.

My experience with this date:

It was a crisp spring evening when Lisa, a girl with whom I had been trying to get in touch with, finally called me back. We had a great conversation and decided to do something fun the next day. "What are we going to do?" she asked. I told her that I would surprise her. The next day she called and wondered if I could find someone to hook her friend, Kelly, up with so we could all go out. I told her that I would and asked one of my good friends, Tony, to go with us. He agreed. We still didn't know what we were going to do at this point, when I thought of Elevator

Tag. It's really good for a blind date atmosphere and, being poor college students at the time, cost was always a consideration.

We picked up the girls and they both looked incredible. They were eager to see what the surprise date was going to be. A deli sandwich place was first for dinner, cheap and very good. It had a fun New York-themed atmosphere and our sandwiches were tasty. My date, Lisa, was nudging my arm, being flirty throughout dinner. I liked that— all very good signs. After eating, us guys let the girls know we were going to play Elevator Tag. They both looked at each other like we were nuts; it was pretty funny. I explained the date to them as we drove to the seven-story building where we would play the game, and Lisa kept up with the flirtatious behavior the entire ride. I couldn't help but smile every time she looked at me or pinched my leg. Queue slow motion sequence, music fades up, "This magic moment . . ."

After we arrived at the building, we split up as couples and the game began. My butt was grabbed a few times on the walk over to the elevators. *Wow, this girl wants me,* I thought and stood a little straighter. My strides became more cowboy-like.

One of the elevators was out of order so, trying to be sneaky, Lisa and I went to the other one and waited there until Tony and Kelly came back to that same floor. They immediately thought we had cheated. We did cheat, but technically we didn't, so they didn't have to know that. We just smiled at our "ability" to pick the right floor. Lisa sat almost on top of me in the car on the way back. It's always nice when a cute girl sits close to you. I was in and I could feel it. My creative date had worked like a charm, and both girls absolutely loved it. However, it wasn't to be, after all.

I'd like to say that Elevator Tag changed my life forever but . . . Lisa never talked to me again. Straight up ghosted me. Why she'd go from grabbing my butt one night to ignoring my calls the next is beyond me, but it's cool—it just meant I was able to hone my creative date skills even further. Silver lining, people. Silver lining.

Creative Date #2

Stargazing: Exploring the Lights Above

Stargazing is fun for a few reasons. You get to lie down and look up at the universe, see an occasional shooting star, and just talk about whatever.

Maybe you'll have a rousing discussion about Aliens and the age-old topic of whether we're alone in the universe. Or some articles about Elon Musk's latest ideas on how to send people to Mars. You could whistle the theme to Star Trek. Get a star map and see how many constellations you can find; there are some pretty cool apps for that. Then look on your arm and see if your freckles form any star formations that match what you see. It totally worked in the movie, *A Beautiful Mind*—he got the girl after that one, no problem. If you've got a telescope, bring it; the date can be done without one, but imagine how cool it'll be to get cheek-to-cheek with your date as you check out the sky through it.

This date isn't just cheap, it's totally free. It allows for good conversation, fresh air, and maybe some cuddle action if you're lucky.

What you need for this date:

For this to be successful, you'll need a few things: blankets, telescope (if you want), pillows, and some treats (there should always be food or drinks of some kind on a date). Location is a key element; choose somewhere with as little light pollution as possible, away from city and neighborhoods. The less light you have around you, the more amazing the stars will look.

My experience with this date:

One amazing weekend while I was enjoying what would be my last summer in Utah, my friend Joey and I decided to go to his cabin. Both of us were interested in this girl named Jessica, so we asked her if she wanted to come with us. If you think two guys to one girl is weird, you're probably right—I guess you could say there was a bit of unstated competition between us to win her affection. We also in invited a couple other guys who would meet us there the next day. Obviously Jessica said yes, considering how cool Joey and I were (cool being a subjective word). We packed our things and set out on our four-wheeling, camping, and gun shooting adventure.

I'll admit I was nervous the entire ride up—I'd had a crush on Jessica ever since I met her a month earlier. She never sent me negative signals and she always said yes when I asked her out. We arrived a few hours later to the rustic cabin, where I immediately hopped on the four-wheeler and went for a ride to go exploring. It didn't even occur to me to ask Jessica to enjoy the ride with me. Lost opportunity.

Since the rest of our group was coming up the next day, we decided to sleep under the stars. In order to get to the grassy meadow we'd chosen, we had to take a four-wheeler, which meant we then had to pile all our gear on it. Three people squished in with a bunch of bedding and supplies at nighttime was probably not the best idea, but we went slowly and cautiously, and arrived safely at the meadow.

The sky was spectacular. I hadn't seen the stars that clear and bright in a long time. The air was cool and fresh, and quite incredible. I didn't have a sleeping bag, so I cuddled up with some blankets, while Jessica curled up in her sleeping bag between me and Joey. We gazed up at the sky, saw spectacular shooting stars, all the while with the full moon shining like a flashlight on us. Of course, I nearly froze to death and didn't sleep a wink because of it, but it was still a remarkable experience.

The next day, our other friends arrived and we spent the day shooting shotguns and riding the four-wheeler. Our friend Jack, who happened to be mine and Joey's roommate, took Jessica out on more than one ride—why didn't I think of that? Smooth, Jack. Smooth. I wasn't a fan of that one, as you can guess. Night came and we sat around the cabin, eating our deer meat stew, joking and laughing and playing cards. The next day we drove home.

Jessica, it turned out, was infatuated with Jack, which Joey and I weren't too happy about. I just love it when your roommate moves in on a girl that you like. Classic. Of course, it wasn't all his fault. It takes two to tango.

Creative Date #3

Let's Go Fly a Kite

Making things together can be a very fun activity to do on a date. Now, don't freak out; I know getting crafty can seem like a lame thing to do, especially to guys. But hear me out.

Something simple to make is a kite. Kites are nostalgic, easy to use, and combine both indoors and outdoors. It is especially nice at the beach, but if you're like most people and don't live near one, a park will do just fine. You could have a picnic afterwards as well, or use glow in the dark paint or attach glow sticks to the kite and then fly it at dark.

If you're like some people I know and absolutely refuse to do something crafty, then go ahead and do it the lazy way; Walmart or Target should sell kites for less than ten dollars. Okay, you're not lazy, you're just a "non-crafter." Forgive me.

What you need for this date:

Kites are simple. All you need are some plastic bags (black garbage bags work well), tape (scotch), string, and balsa wood (which will make up the kite's frame). The balsa wood can be bought for really cheap at a hobby store. You could also use long wooden dowel rods.

The frame should be made first. The simplest and most classic kite frame style is the T, or cross frame. The size is up to you. Smaller kites do not fly that well, so 3' long by 2' wide seems to be ideal, although I've seen some as big as 8' long and 6' wide. Assemble the kite, and don't forget the tail at the end; a streamer or ribbon should do the trick for that. Slightly windy days work best for this date, so you'll have to do it at the right time.

(See diagram below)

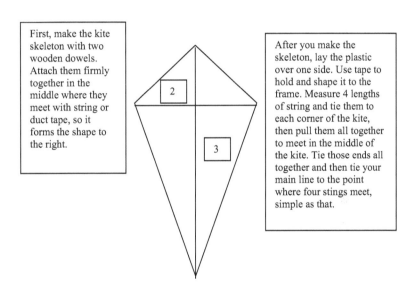

First, make the kite skeleton with two wooden dowels. Attach them firmly together in the middle where they meet with string or duct tape, so it forms the shape to the right.

After you make the skeleton, lay the plastic over one side. Use tape to hold and shape it to the frame. Measure 4 lengths of string and tie them to each corner of the kite, then pull them all together to meet in the middle of the kite. Tie those ends all together and then tie your main line to the point where four stings meet, simple as that.

My commentary on this date:

I made several kites in my younger years. On one particular date I had with my friend, she put her crafting skills to work and we wound up making one that was so big it took both of us just to fly it. We even had to use rope instead of string just to hold up our behemoth. It was pretty clever on my part, insisting it be bigger— a good excuse to be super close to her. There were soft touches, flirty glances; it was totally worth the crafty effort.

Since then, I've visited many beaches and parks where couples looking to be on a date were flying a kite, watching it soar through the air with smiles, laughing and having a good time. Kite flying does seem like it was something more popular decades ago, but it doesn't have to be—it's time to start a revolution, my friends. Grab a date, make or buy a kite, then go fly it. You could even break out sing that famous song from the movie, *Mary Poppins*: "Let's go fly a kite, up to the highest height, up in the atmosphere, up where the air is clear, oh let's go fly a kite!"

Creative Date #4

A Picnic/Walk in the Park

Since the olden days, a classic date has always been a picnic in the park; a contrast from today's common dinner and a movie. Why not go back to a simpler time and take her on a picnic?

Food is easy. Sandwiches are classic, and with all the sandwich shops nowadays, you don't even have to make them yourself. Grab some soda, and men, here's a tip—don't forget treats. Don't you *ever* forget to pack treats. Something homemade might even earn you some bonus points in the form of a kiss. It's science.

Location is key. Pick a dinky park right next to a loud intersection and you've just got an awkward hour together. Pick a quiet park next to a duck-filled lake and you've got several hours of shy glances, touching her hand, giggles, and precious moments. Why is this such a good date? Well, there's nature, there's low-cost, and there's also something to be said about the simplicity of it. Picnics don't need frills or complications. It's just you, your date, nature, and a blanket. Awesome.

What you need for this date:

You need the food, a blanket to sit on, and a stellar location. You can also bring a Frisbee, a kite, a football, or even cards. If there's a lake nearby, bring some bread to feed the ducks.

My experience with this date:

I have done this one a lot; it's one of my go-to dates. And one of them stands out in particular, with a girl named Dawn. I wasn't looking for anything extravagant, just wanting to have some basic interaction, seeing as we didn't know each other all that well yet. We went and picked up sandwiches from her favorite lunch place, then stopped at the local park. And before you ask, yes, I had treats. Of course I did.

After eating, we played the questions game, which basically entails asking each other—you guessed it— random, funny questions. We seemed to have a lot in common, there wasn't any forced conversation, no awkward pauses, and, as a bonus, she was super pretty. But . . . love is a finicky thing. Even though she seemed really interested, it just didn't click for me, and I'm still not sure why. Love is just weird, I guess.
We all want it to click for both people. Really click; the kind of click where you just sit and think, "This is too good to be true." And sometime is *does* end up being too good to be true. Or you get lucky, and wind up living happily ever after.

Creative Date #5

A Nice Sunday drive (or Saturday, or whenever you feel like it)

Sometimes it's nice to get in your car and take a drive around the countryside, city, or along the coast; whatever scenery fits your style. Having a convertible makes it even better— put the top down and enjoy the wind in your hair, if you have hair . . . I personally don't, but I do remember the feeling fondly. Grab a date, and venture forth to some cool destination. Oh and if you are feeling crazy adventurous get out an actual map and travel by that. Yeah a map, remember those folded up pieces of paper with all the ink marks on it tucked away in some dark corner of your glove compartment? Resist the urge to use your smart phone, and maybe even stop and ask for directions—a novel idea, I know. Get a blend of fresh air and pleasant scenery. Blast some music and sing along to it.

The natural landscape that the world has to offer is an incredible setting for a date. Most people really do enjoy the cliché things like seascapes, purple mountains, and amber waves of grain. Sunsets, sun rises, crystal blue lakes, white tipped peaks, and all the critters that can be seen in their natural habitats. This sort of date would be perfect for the city folk who don't get out to nature very often.

It is really easy to find a national or state park in your area; just go online and search for one. Within a few minutes you'll have several places to drive to, and don't forget a map—remember, no cell phones! Oh okay, you can bring one if you like. Fancy castles? Go online and look for neighborhoods near you that have them, then drive over and take pictures. One place to look is http://www.dupontcastle.com/castles/, a site that lists Castles in different states—and yeah, even places like Arizona have them. Being a bit of a giddy nerd when it comes to castles, it's one site I might search through to find an interesting destination.

In California, the Pacific Coast Highway is an excellent drive, whether you go 10 miles or 300. The Hearst Castle is located right off of it in a town called San Simeon. The tours there are pretty awesome and would add some culture to your coastal drive. I'm guessing the majority of you don't live near the coast, but no biggie— a drive through the mountains is really nice, too.

What you need for this date:

This is an inexpensive date that requires only transportation and an idea of where you want to go. If you plan to take a tour to one of the well-known castles, you might want to look at the website or get a number to see if you'll need to reserve tickets, and I think I mentioned something about bringing a map.

My commentary on this date:

I've driven through a variety of amazing locales, and through some of the most breathtaking national parks with my family and friends, making happy, exciting memories. It was a perfect time for deep and light conversation, a time for car games like, *I Spy with my little eye*, a time for jokes, and a time to just relax. Can't think of something to do for your next date? Well, my friends, here's an idea—go for a drive.

Creative Date #6

Scrapbooking

Is Scrapbooking dead in this digital age? It doesn't have to be. Plenty of stores like Michaels or Hobby Lobby still carry loads of scrapbooking supplies. A fun and cheap idea for a date would be to put together a scrapbook with pictures of you and your significant other together. More of the time, the girls are the ones most interested in this (Shocking? Nope.). Surprise her by showing interest in it as well.

You'll need supplies; most likely an album and paper, and probably all those cutesy, sparkly stickers and embellishments. Oh yeah, and then there's the pictures. Go through your ten thousand-plus photos and pick a handful to scrapbook. And yeah, a crafty date might sound crazy to some, but trust me, the brownie points that will be won are well worth it. While you're at it, make some brownies, too—remember that whole treats idea?

What you need for this date:

An album, scissors, pictures, and anything to make it more interesting, like embellishments. And just in case you didn't hear me the first time—don't forget treats.

My commentary on this date:

In the movie "Bruce Almighty," Jennifer Aniston's character tries in vain to get Jim Carrey's character to scrapbook with her, and finally at the end of the movie he makes a scrapbook all by himself. He really should have just sucked it up and made the dang craft with her in the first place. A lost opportunity, but he made up for it with a surprise gift and won her heart in the end. Remember, this date is a very inexpensive way to have fun and reminisce the past, not to mention creating something that no doubt you both will treasure.

Creative Date #7

Free Food Date

Something you could do on a Saturday afternoon is what I refer to as the "Free Food Date". Basically you drive around to all the stores you know give out free samples. Yeah, it's simple, but it's fun, it's free, and you can bring some competition into the day; make a game out of it and see who can get the most freebies.

A great store to do this at is Costco. And don't just make one round; go around again and get seconds. If the sample worker gives you a funny look, or asks "Haven't you gotten one already?" say yes—there's no need to lie, it just makes it funnier if they're weirded out. Maybe even throw an accent in there.

There are probably other places that give out free food samples, and if you know about them you could go there as well. And if it just so happens to be your birthday, there are several places where you can go and they will give you free food.

What you need for this date:

You don't need anything special for this idea, just a few locations in mind, then drive over and feast on the free food.

My commentary on this date:

Every time I'm in Costco I think this would be fun to do for a date. I mean, I enjoy doing it alone or with friends and family, so why not with a girl? It would be a totally free date, not to mention it could potentially be really funny, depending on who is working the sample stands, and how many times you try to get freebies from each stand.

Creative Date #8

Care to Karaoke?

Take your date to a place that has karaoke and show off your singing skills . . . or lack thereof. Whether or not you're an excellent singer doesn't matter. Is anyone really a good singer that does karaoke? There may be a few, but for the most part it's just fun to be up there and jam. You could have the music track prepared for a song that you wrote on a thumb drive and then give it to the DJ and have him play it while you sing to your date—talk about impressive. Maybe you can get your date up there and sing a song together; a classic duet like *Baby it's Cold Outside,* or *Don't Know Much*. Whether it's a group date or just the two of you, get ready for a fun-filled night of rockin' out.

What you need for this date:

It's pretty simple; just find a place in your area that has karaoke. That's what Google is for, right? You could also get a bit crazy and dress up as your favorite singers, give the crowd a good laugh and sing something funny, or blow their minds with the most amazing rendition they have ever heard.

My experience with this date:

A while ago, my friend planned a house party with food, games, and yes, Karaoke. My friend Leslie and I decided to sing a duet, and we straight-up crushed *A Whole New World*, from the movie *Aladdin*. When the song ended we were given enthusiastic applause, of course, and plenty of praise. Nailed it. I've never taken Leslie on an actual date after that night, but maybe I should; with our skills, we could go to some Karaoke bar and bring the house down. Mic drop.

On another occasion, I took a date dancing to a country bar and grill, where Karaoke was one of the attractions. We watched and listened to other couples and solo singers, but didn't sing ourselves. I might have taken the leap and jumped up to the karaoke plate and sung . . . if I'd had more interest in my date, that is.

I tend to think that you have to really be interested in the person if you're willing to sing in front of a bunch of people you don't know, especially if you aren't the best singer. However, you might have the type of personality where it doesn't matter who you're with or what kind of audience you have—when the Karaoke machine calls, you answer.

Creative Date #9

Nature's Hot Tub

Some areas of the United States, along with other parts of the world, have some very intriguing natural hot springs that are excellent for a date. You can do it day or night, just as long as you know where they are. Hot springs are not usually an easy thing to get to, and some hiking will probably be involved, but it's worth it.

Nature's hot tub is a good way to describe these pools of goodness. Iceland is actually famous for its hot springs; they attract people from all over the world. Now I'm not suggesting you have to go to Iceland to find some, although that *would* be quite the date to remember. If you don't already know where a hot spring is, you can find one close to you with a simple search on the web. The biggest draw about this awesome date is that it's more adventurous than using the classic, boring, residential-style hot tub.

What you need for this date:

This is another free date, besides the gas money, unless you choose to go to a tourist attraction hot spring where you pay to get in. Those aren't as adventurous, in my opinion; they're set up like swimming pools and are way more crowded and touristy, but they can definitely still be enjoyable. Depending on the location of the springs, you could sit in the water and look up at the stars, listen to the wildlife, and maybe even tell a scary story or two.

Transportation is all you need for this date. Type in the address in your smart phone and be on your way. If you go at nighttime make sure to have flashlights. And what is a good adventure without food? Make sure to pack something yummy, and don't ever forget the treats.

My commentary on this date:

In the past I have always gone to hot springs with family or friends. The one in Ouray, Colorado is really nice, but it's one of those pay-to-enter places, and is more like a swimming pool heated by the spring. There are several hot springs here in Arizona where I live. One popular location is the Verde Hot Spring, near Camp Verde. I was invited to go with a group to this hot spring, but unfortunately I was not able to go. I was jealous when I heard the stories of the wondrous place, and not to mention I missed out on meeting the cute girls that went on the trip. It is actually quite the adventure to get to that location: the hiking trail is not clearly marked, and you have to ford the river or bring a raft or tube to get across. But even with the sketchy journey, from the stories I heard, the hot springs are well worth the effort.

Hot tubs are a very popular thing in America, and when you take the beauty of nature and the warm soothing sensation of water, you have a recipe for a fun, relaxing evening with a touch of adventure. Bring a date and make it romantic, or bring a group for more fun!

Creative Date #10

Winter's Tent

A really exciting winter activity is building a snow cave. If you are super ambitious you can make one that will fit your whole group to sleep in, or you can make a small cozy one just for the two of you.

Snow caving is quite easy, and honestly, this date might save your life—who knows when you'll be in a survival situation where you'd need intricate knowledge of snow cave making. Happens all the time, right? Okay fine, maybe not. But still, basically building a fort out of snow is pretty awesome.

This doesn't have to be a freezing evening. Snow caves are remarkably warm inside because they capture your body heat and hold it inside the structure. Also, you won't have to worry too much about it falling apart, as the cool air outside keeps the snow cave together. Bear Grylls and Les Stroud will be proud of you. In case you don't know who they are, they are the stars of *Man vs. Wild* and *Survivor Man*. Those guys are epic.

What you need for this date:

You need snow and probably want to be up in the mountains where it's more fun. Shovels are a must for this operation and snow shovels are ideal, but even standard ones will work. Buckets will make it easier as well.

There are a couple of techniques that can be used for making a snow cave. The first technique is to shovel a ton of snow until the pile is about 4 to 6 feet high, and pack it together. The bigger the pile, the better the cave will be. Next, start at the bottom and slowly remove the inside of the pile out. Make sure to leave about two feet of thickness for the roof and sides otherwise it will be too weak and collapse.

The second method for this requires using branches to form a frame and then piling snow all around it. Either way works great. This date is totally free, unless you buy snow shovels, and of course it will probably cost you a little gas money to get to the location.

My experience with this date:

The first winter I was in Utah, years ago for college, two of my best buddies, John and Tim, who were also my roommates at the time, decided to get a group of people together and go snow caving. I remembered doing it with the Boy Scouts a long time ago and thought it would be fun to do in college. Another friend of ours, Jason, said he was going to meet us there and that he would bring some girls up, too, to which I agreed would be a great idea. It wasn't planned as a date, but Jason had a crush on one of the girls he was bringing.

The location was only about an hour away from our apartment and happened to be a normal campground that was covered in snow. We started building our snow cave around 5 in the afternoon and worked well into the night. We made an enormous cave. The entrance was small, just big enough to crawl through and then it opened up into a cavern. And seriously . . . it was amazing.

We hung out in our little winter house for a few hours before someone had the bright idea to try and make the cave larger by digging away from the ceiling. Sure enough, it collapsed on us, but we could only laugh. So you can learn from our little mistake that the number one rule for snow caving is to not make the ceiling too thin. We decided that that was the end of that, packed up, and left for an actual house where we played card games and drank hot chocolate.

Creative Date #11

Explore a Museum

For a cultured experience, take your date to a museum. There are all sorts you can go to, with interesting exhibits ranging from everything like Egyptian, dinosaur, and air and space. Museums are great because you get to learn cool stuff about, well, cool stuff. Plus, you automatically feel kind of special and sophisticated going inside a museum, almost like your IQ just went up 20 points.

Take your date back in time and look at what American History has to offer, or visit some world history museum and learn more about ancient civilizations. It works well as a group activity or with just the two of you, and it is a perfect first date idea. It may not be the most active thing to do, but it is definitely worth going. Some museums are free, and while others may have an admission price, it's usually a nominal fee, similar to the price of a movie ticket for some, while others are in the 20-dollar range. Washington D.C. has some spectacular museums, same with San Francisco—in general, large cities will almost surely have a museum of some kind. And while you're in museum mode, why not follow up the experience by sitting down and watching *Night at the Museum*? Ben Stiller is a perfect way to cap off the day.

What you need for this date:

Just like a lot of activities, all you need is a time and place to go. Reservations are usually not required.

My experience with this date:

I have been to many different kinds of museums, from the Dinosaur Museum in Utah, to the Fine Arts Museums of San Francisco, and the Smithsonian National Air and Space Museum in Washington D.C. I recently took a date to the Arizona Science Center; they had a murder mystery activity going on with a High School Reunion, 80's themed. Most of the patrons came dressed in their best 80's attire, so you know how totally radical it was. There was a crime scene to explore, clues to discover, fingerprint analysis, handwriting analysis, blood splatter analysis, not to mention all the normal exhibits the center had to offer.

There was a break out session as well, where the head of the forensics department of one of the local colleges spoke to us about the impact TV shows like *CSI* and *Bones* have on real life injuries. It was a fascinating topic for sure. After reviewing all of the clues brilliantly, my date and I deduced whom the murderer was. A great first date!

Creative Date #12

Serve It Up!

If you and your date are in a "giving" mood, you could do a service activity together. Some ideas could be volunteering at a soup kitchen at Christmas time, or maybe you could set up a free car wash for a few hours. You could go to one of your neighbor's houses, maybe an elderly couple's home, and do yard work for them, and then afterwards have a water fight to clean off. Feed My Starving Children is an excellent place to do some good will. Service activities are always really fun for those involved, and no matter how messy or tired you get, you always wind up feeling great inside afterwards.

What you need for this date:

You don't need much for this to be successful, only your willingness to serve others, your time, and whatever supplies you'll need, depending on the project you'll be doing. https://www.justserve.org/ is a great place to find service projects.

My commentary on this date:

Growing up, I had the opportunity to do a lot of service projects in group settings, and there was usually a girl there that I had some interest in beyond friendship. That's not the main reason why I was there, in case you're wondering if I'm just a womanizer. Flirting while doing good to others is just an added perk, right?

During one group project in particular, everyone involved had a smashing good time and the recipients of the service were thrilled. I remember going to and elderly woman's house and our group picked weeds, mowed her front yard, pruned the trees, raked leaves and ground clutter, among other things. Afterwards, the yard looked immaculate and the woman was so grateful. I felt pretty good after that, cute girls or not.

Creative Date #13

I Ain't Afraid of No Ghost Town

Scooby Dooby Doo, where are you? If you're a fan of adventuring and exploring and your date is somewhat interested in the idea, take a trip to a nearby ghost town. Not only can you learn some really neat historical stuff about the town, you can turn it into a pretty creepy event. And yeah, creeping out your date is absolutely fun and appropriate. These are creative dates, people!

This would be something fun to do around Halloween. If you planned it right, you could have a different group of people show up early to the ghost town and hide, making noises and doing all sorts of funny things to scare your date. Make up some story of your own about how the place got haunted. Maybe a convict escaped a nearby prison and was said to be living in the town or something like that. It's always fun to test just how gullible your date is.

Another idea would be to film the two of you with your smart phone and turn it into one of those cheesy ghost hunter shows. You could bring a real video camera and film your own horror movie, or have a hidden cameraperson recording the date who then surprises you later and watches the video with you. Depending on where the Ghost Town is located, you could even turn it into a whole night event by camping out on the outskirts of town, huddled around a small fire, roasting marshmallows and telling scary stories.

What you need for this date:

First you need to find a ghost town. Probably the best place to find one is at http://www.ghosttowns.com/ Kind of a clever name, I know. It's a pretty comprehensive list and allows you to find exactly what you want close to home or far away. Next you need food, which you can pack or buy along the way. Sleeping arrangements should be made beforehand if you'll be sleeping overnight, and whether at a motel or on the side of the road, you need to have the appropriate gear with you, like sleeping bags, pillows, tents, etc.

My commentary on this date:

I have researched this idea pretty thoroughly. My fascination with the horror genre and ghost towns in general is legit, and is what served as the inspiration for this date. Doesn't it just seem like something straight out of a horror movie? Awesome, I know. I have had plenty of people who've done this tell me how scary and fun it was being in a real-life ghost town. If planned correctly and attention is paid to details, this could wind up being one of the most exhilarating dates you've been on. The person you're with will definitely appreciate the time and effort that was put into creating this adventurous activity.

Creative Date #14

Books for Days

For a relaxing and intellectual evening, take your date to the local library. Each of you pick out one of your favorite books, then find a spot on a couch and cuddle up for some reading. You could borrow a movie if you wanted, then go home and watch it with some popcorn.

Bookstores like Barnes and Noble are good for dates like this as well. You could get some food at the café there and then each pick out a magazine or book to read. At the end of the night, you can even buy the book for her for as a present. The beauty of this date is that you can make it as cheap as you want, if not totally free.

What you need for this date:

You don't need anything for this besides a library card if you plan to check anything out.

My commentary on this date:

I went to the library a lot with my family and friends growing up. Those were some pretty fun times. Reading good books and being with good company always makes for a stimulating and relaxing time.

In college, one of the popular places to meet people to ask out on a date was the periodicals section of the library. There were numerous stories about how a girl and guy met in that part of the library and ended up getting married. Kind of funny, I was always under the impression that girls studying or reading didn't want to be bothered, but hey, no guts no glory. And whoever says a library isn't a romantic place is just plain wrong—I'd always see couples at libraries holding hands, cuddling, and enjoying their time together. It's got a great ambiance for that kind of thing.

The idea behind this is similar to the museum date; getting to know some of their interests while also having good conversation. If you have kids, it could just be a pleasant quiet evening away by yourselves, as well.

Creative Date #15

Downtown, Where All the Lights are Bright

For a fun and adventurous date, take a drive to the City. For example, if I lived in San Jose, I could take a drive to San Francisco. While there, I might do the awesome touristy things like Pier 39, Alcatraz, or Lombard Street. There's always so much to do in huge cities that you could spend days there.

This can be especially fun if your date grew up in a small town and doesn't get to go to big cities that often. When you get hungry, you're in luck—big cities have everything from street food to fancy places a food snob goes crazy for. Go to the best restaurant in town, or find some old mom and pop restaurant. Afterwards, you could ride the elevator in the tallest skyscraper, or take a tour of one of the historical buildings, like the Empire State Building, Coit Tower, or maybe the Space Needle. Don't forget to do some people watching while you're at it; you're bound to see all sorts of interesting folks downtown (in other words, the crazies).

What you need for this date:

Get the car keys, fill up on gas (depending on how far you have to go), and enjoy. Take pictures with your phone or camera so you can preserve the memories.

My experience with this date:

I've taken girls downtown a lot. It's one of those dates that will never get old. One time, a friend of mine set me up on a blind date with a girl named Jill. I told her we would take a trip downtown and be spontaneous when we were there. I knew she would like the spontaneous bit, because duh, who wouldn't? Okay . . . maybe my friend told me that Jill would like it. But still, spontaneous is always good.

Blind dates usually aren't my favorite thing in the world, but I am always open to the idea. I picked up Jill and immediately got more excited—she was super cute and seemed really awesome. We drove downtown and walked around the outdoor mall they had. The mall was incredible, probably one of the best I've been to. Jill was being flirty with me so I flirted back; everything was playing out well.

After a lunch of quality Chinese food, she wanted to see a movie, which I don't usually like to do on a first date. But since things were going so well, I didn't object. Part of my excitement *may* have been the prospect of holding hands in the dark. And I was right. We held hands, she flirted, it was great.

But seeing as love is weird, as the date went on, I slowly began to decide she might not be the one for me. By the time we got home, I'd lost interest. Dumb? Maybe. She was cute, smart, fun to be with, and liked a lot of the things I liked. It just happened to be another episode where a cool girl liked me but for some reason I didn't. I hate it when that happens.

This particular date was a little more expensive than it could have been. However, when you visit downtown you don't have to spend any money if you don't want to, maybe very little at all. It all depends on what activities you wind up doing there. Overall it was a very fun experience even though the outcome was not exactly a perfect one.

Creative Date #16

The Questions Game

The questions game is a brilliant get-to-know-you type date and is very simple. It could be over lunch or in the park, or maybe at night on your way to a movie.

      The game is simple: each of you takes turns asking each other creative questions in order to get to know them better. I've done this on first dates a couple of times, and it works pretty well. You can ask questions like, "What was your favorite cartoon growing up?" or "If you were going to be stranded on an island, what three things would you have with you?" That one is my favorite question to ask; it's interesting what weird things people say they'll bring. Other types of questions could be "this or that" questions. For example, "Pancakes or waffles?" Get a little more creative and ask things like, "Cleaning toilets or organizing a sock drawer?" The key is to make sure a new question is asked each time, so if you like their question you can ask them the same one back, but then you still need to ask a new question after.

What you need for this date:

You don't need anything. This is absolutely free. You could pick your date up and just go for a nice walk around a park or neighborhood and ask the questions. It's that simple.

My experience with this date:

I've done this a few times, and probably the best time I had was years ago during Christmas vacation while in college. I heard there was a group of people meeting up for an activity, so being the enthusiast that I am, I decided to attend. I saw a rather attractive girl with a friend of mine, so I went and introduced myself to her. Her name was Jenny and she happened to be that friend's new roommate. Nice, lucky me. We seemed to hit it off pretty well during the five minutes of waiting around for the group to show up.

The night's activity was board games and twister. Being fond of board games I was excited to see how the night's activities would unfold. I decided to play twister and Jenny thankfully decided to join in. Being the incredibly inflexible person that I am, I lost every time. There were a couple important things I learned that night, however: don't wear jeans while playing twister, and that Jenny liked to play video games. At the end of the night, I gave her a ride home, since she lived in the same condominium complex as me, and invited her over to test her XBOX skills.

We didn't play very long, but she wasn't kidding when she said she liked video games; she could definitely hold her own. Afterward, I suggested the questions game, and we talked into the early morning. She was digging me. We actually dated after that for a little while, but then for some reason it didn't feel right. I was totally attracted to her, we had a lot in common, but the deep connection was not there. Surface connection, yes, but not the type I was looking for, and she felt the same way in the end. So ultimately it wound up working out for the best.

Creative Date #17

Get Your Sweat On

Picture this: music fades in, and it's one of the most iconic workout songs of all time, *Eye of the Tiger*. It plays with unabashed intensity; you smile at your date as you tie your shoelaces, and then take a long swig of water. You both set off on a jog around the neighborhood, or some scenic running trail. Not many words are spoken; you just enjoy each other's company as you burn the calories from last night's glorious dinner and the slice of cheesecake you felt both guilty and not guilty about eating.

As you can probably guess, for this date idea, go and sweat your guts out! Running, the gym, rock climbing—even a fun aerobics class. I am not joking when I say this idea works really well with the right person. Is the gym not your thing? There's always paddleboats or even just swimming at the lake. If you're feeling up for a challenge, take a spin class together (those things are legit), or do some yoga. If you're trying to get back into shape, it's much easier to stay motivated when the object of your heart's desire is right there beside you doing the same thing.

What you need for this date:

This one is pretty simple; head to your local gym, running trail, or down your neighborhood streets. It all depends on the location and activity you choose.

My commentary with this date:

I frequent the gym quite a bit, and I constantly see couples working out together. It's something I really enjoy, so why wouldn't I want a cute girl there with me? I can't think of a better spotter than my crush as I pump some iron on the bench press, looking down at me with her amazing eyes or holding my feet as I do crunches. Pretty darn awesome if you ask me. I've also taken girls on dates to a rock climbing place on several occasions and had a blast each time. But I have a whole date idea surrounding the indoor climbing gym, so I won't spoil it here.

Creative Date #18

Visit the Old Folks Home: Bingo, Anyone?

If you're feeling in a particularly giving mood, take your date to an old folk's home. They are the sweetest people and really do enjoy having visitors.

You don't even have to know anyone that lives there; all you need is the willingness to have fun. Some things that you can do with them include playing cards or other games like bingo. Play music and dance with them, sing songs, play an instrument—whatever you want. You'll truly make them happy, and will leave feeling pretty good on the inside. If you happen to have a relative there, even better.

What you need for this date:

I would call ahead and make sure that it's alright to visit first. You could bring a group with you if you wanted, or have it be just the two of you.

My commentary on this date:

I have visited old folk's homes before as groups. On one occasion years ago, I had a bit of a crush on a girl named Heather in the group. I'd planned it perfectly so I could ride with her to the home. After getting there, we spent about an hour talking with the people in the activities center. We wheeled them back and forth from their rooms, and dropped by the bed-ridden folks' rooms to chat with them a bit as well. We played games, and even danced with them. I remember this one lady who could still move pretty well for an eighty-five-year-old; she told me that she hadn't danced for over twenty years and that she really appreciated the chance to bust a move with a "nice young fellow."

While there I would glance once in a while at Heather and she would give me a smile—a flirty one, I might add. Yes, I can tell the difference. It's a gift. I left the home feeling quite happy; not just because I knew Heather was digging me, but also because I knew the people there really enjoyed having us come and visit them. Some of them hadn't had visitors in over a year. Giving back really is great, isn't it?

During that next week I asked Heather to go to a musical with me, and she said that she was kind of seeing someone and didn't know if they were exclusive or not, but that she would call me back the next day to let me know if she could go. She didn't call back until Thursday, which was the day right before the date, only to tell me that she better not go. Ummm, news flash to everyone: don't wait until the last second to tell someone you can't make a date. It's a tad on the rude side. Oh well, such is life.

More recently I met up with a large group of singles that put together and activity to play bingo with the elderly at one of the local homes. It was a good mix of single guys and girls, and I met someone that I ended up taking out.

Creative Date #19

Brown Baggin' It

One way to see how much your date pays attention to the things you say is to plan an activity that involves eating lunch, but in brown-bag form.

What you do is tell them to pack a lunch and that you will do the same, except that you'll be making them for each other. When you get to the park, beach, mountains, or wherever, you exchange lunches and see if your date likes what you got them. You might include things like their favorite gum or candy bar, favorite type of sandwich, chips, etc. This is something different than going to a restaurant and is a unique twist to the whole picnic idea. The cost is minimal for this as well and could definitely be done in a group setting. If there *are* several people, you could put all the lunches in the middle and then sit around them in a circle, play some sort of game, and the winner gets to pick a lunch first, and so on and so forth until everyone has a lunch. To be funny, put something odd in there. But nothing too crazy—you don't want anyone to starve, so make sure everything is edible. If you're still not convinced of this idea, I can assure you, it's a great way to spend an afternoon and get some laughs while you're at it.

What you need for this date:

You need a brown bag, food, and a place to go.

My commentary on this date:

The idea for this date stems from my fondness for white elephant gift exchanges. The humor is usually priceless, and the frantic behavior of people trying to get an actual good gift is hilarious. The pouting of those who once had a cool gift but are now deprived of a present fairy tales are made of all bring a smile to my face.

I have participated in many of these exchanges, and since I love food, thought it would be both an excellent cheap group date, as well as a romantic activity with just you and that special someone. The response for this particular date activity is pretty much the same as with the white elephant gift exchange, but with even more enthusiasm because it is a great twist on a popular tradition that most people haven't done before.

Creative Date #20

Country Dancing

One of my favorite cheaper date ideas is to take a girl country dancing. I actually go quite a bit, usually every Wednesday night.

There are all kinds of venues that you can choose. There are country bar and grills, like Dierks Bentley's Whiskey Row, Toby Keith's restaurant, or other more specific dance club venues. Usually there is a small cover charge to get in, but some of the country bars are actually free. I don't particularly love country music, but I do enjoy it while dancing. The place I go to regularly has an hour lesson before the main dancing begins which is awesome, especially if you or your date don't really know how to dance.

Country dancing or just dancing in general is a great way to get to know your date, and even get some people-watching in at the same time.

What you need for this date:

All you need is to find a place to go. Just Google "country dancing in my area" and you'll see many options come up.

My experience with this date:

I have done this date a few times; it is one of my go-to activities. Recently, I took a girl out for some barbeque, then walked across the street for an incredible dessert, and ended up at a country bar for some dancing. The area was awesome— downtown Gilbert, Arizona, full of restaurants and activities all within walking distance of each other. We danced, laughed, talked, people-watched and had a great time. We even wound up going out on a second date.

Creative Date #21

Touring the Galaxy and Beyond

Before you judge, let me just tell you—planetariums are cooler than you think.

One of the local community colleges where I live happens to have an amazing one. Each first Friday of the month they have "Astronomy Nights," where they open up their planetarium to the public and have really cool free shows every half hour. One of my favorites is "Tour the Universe with Pink Floyd." Basically, it's a universe exploration show set to some of Pink Floyd's classic songs. They also usually have telescopes set up outside pointed at the moon or a planet. How cool is that?

This activity is an awesome date idea, especially if your date likes astronomy. Check your local colleges to see if they have something similar, or you can visit the nearest Observatory to you. Each will usually have a website with their calendar or events posted. Not only is this date super interesting, it gets bonus points for being cheap.

What you need for this date:

You really just need to find out where to go. It is probably a good idea to get there early for tickets; I know they tend to go really fast at the one I mentioned near me.

My experience with this date:

I have gone on dates to the first Friday planetarium shows a few times, and they were always a success.

On one particular occasion, I went with a girl named Tiffany. Right after I picked her up, I wrote names of a few restaurants on pieces of paper and put them in a bowl for her to draw out. She wound up picking Mimi's Café, which is a great place to eat. Afterward, we headed over to the planetarium. We talked and talked the entire time in both the ticket line and in our seats as we waited for the show to start. I was giddy with anticipation, and not only because of Tiffany; I just love astronomy shows!

Finally we were let in and found some great seats. The lights dimmed and our universe tour began. I don't think my smile ever left my face during the 25-minute presentation. I glanced at Tiffany a few times during the show and it was obvious she was having just as good of a time as I was. Although we wound up not being a match for each other, it was still a lot of fun, and visiting the planetarium is still one of my favorite creative date ideas!

Creative Date #22

House Hunting

One of my hobbies is to drive around on an early-evening weekday or a Saturday morning and visit the new-build neighborhoods.

The reason I like it so much is probably because I'm a dreamer—right now I live in an old townhome, and I can't wait to buy a single-family residence. I enjoy looking at all the different floor plans and upgrades; there are so many amazing options out there. Every once in a while, there will be a super fancy new neighborhood with enormous estates/mansions that are even more fun to explore. Probably because I'll realistically never end up in one of those, but hey, a guy can dream, right?

This would be a fun date to do even if you are not in the market to buy a new home. And the houses don't have to be brand new builds; you could find an old mansion for sale and go to the open house, tour some tiny houses, or whatever peaks your interest. So if you're looking for something to do on the weekend, grab a date and go look at some houses!

What you need for this date:

All you need to make this date happen is some housing developments to explore, open houses to investigate, etc. You may want to combine this with another date idea like a picnic beforehand or something like that.

My experience with this date:

Several years ago I took a girl on a date down to the Tucson, AZ area. They were having an event where a new development of mansions was open for touring. We drove down there and explored all of the amazingly huge homes. It was a super fun experience. It didn't even matter that I wasn't in the market at the time; I couldn't afford those houses if I *was* looking to buy.

More recently I've gone around with my friend and his wife as they've been house hunting, and explored every type of home from the small and bland to the enormous and immaculate. I love seeing all the different styles and sizes . . . until I remember how I bought my townhome at the peak of the market and it's just barely worth more than I owe on it. That reminder sucks, big time. Even more so knowing that same friend bought a unit in my complex at the bottom of the market. He's got like 100k equity now. Score for him, depression for me. In fact, I think I actually threw up a little bit in my mouth just thinking about it. Kidding.

Chapter 2: Group Dates

The More the Merrier

There is one simple truth that exists in dating: sometimes, dates are just more fun with a group of people.

In fact, some ideas actually require that you have more than two people involved. Group dates not only create a fun atmosphere that includes everyone, you're also usually in for a bit of comedy relief throughout the date. With that many personalities involved, you're bound to have a good laugh. Also, groups tend to be really good first date opportunities, as it's a chance to get to know someone in a low-pressure environment.

Creative Date #23

Murder Mystery Dinner Party

A murder mystery dinner is a party that allows the participants to remove themselves from everyday life. Some might say it's nerdy, but I'd call it more of an escapism, if you will.

One of the best parts of this is that everyone gets to be a completely different person for a night. They put on their thinking/sleuth caps to solve a murder. How fun is that? Mystery parties have been a popular form of entertainment for many years; in fact, murder mystery parties date back to the parlor games of Medieval Europe. The basic idea is that everyone is given a character identity for the evening—characters with backstory and who are acquainted with one of the other characters who's been killed. The participants then spend the evening acting as their characters while trying to figure out who committed the murder, where they did it, and how they did it. The twist is that all the guests have motives, so it is quite possible that any one of them could be the murderer.

Dressing up for the part will help you get in the acting mood and adds a really fun element to the night. I have never met someone who didn't like a murder mystery party. It's kind of like the game *CLUE,* but you get to act it out instead of playing it as a board game.

What you need for this date:

In order for this to work, you need a murder mystery kit. You can buy these at hobby shops, online, eBay, etc., or if you are creative and a good writer and storyteller, you can write your own. These games typically involve eight people, four women and four men, so it is a perfect group date activity. You don't have to plan it around dinner but it works the best if you have a three-course meal prepared so people can have something to do while acting the night out.

My experience with this date:

I've done this date idea several times, and it's always a blast. Here is my first experience with a Murder Mystery Dinner Party: One summer, I was on an eBay kick, so I would haunt garage sales and search for stuff I knew I could sell online for a lot more than I would have to pay for it. While I was rummaging through the goods at one particular house, I found a never-been-opened Murder Mystery Party kit. Talk about a great find! I had always wanted to try one of those and here was an unopened kit in perfect condition. I quickly snatched it up and paid one dollar for it. I was incredibly stoked, considering they go for about thirty dollars brand new in the store. I could've put it on eBay and made money, but I didn't sell this treasure. I used it to plan my first Murder Mystery Dinner Party.

Some time later I had a chance to actually do the party. I was dating this particular girl with whom I wanted to elevate the status from friends to "more than friends," if you know what I mean. This would be our fifth formal date and things seemed to be going well. She was bright, energetic, and very easy on the eyes, and her smile could light up even the darkest of rooms. She liked to have fun and I knew a Murder Mystery Dinner Party would be a big hit. We planned the evening's event at her mom's house (a two bedroom, four man bachelor apartment doesn't exactly have a true dining room for a real dinner party, but you can improvise with card tables, coffee tables, and counters, if you have no other options).

Everyone arrived buzzing with excitement for the event. They were dressed up as if they truly were a character in a mystery novel. To start off the event right, everyone had researched their assigned roles so they'd be comfortable and know what to do. I prepared, cooked, and served a three-course meal for all of us, which consisted of salad, shredded pork barbecue sandwiches, and banana and strawberry splits.

Conversation during dinner was electric as everyone played his or her roles and tried to solve the mystery. My date was particularly attractive that night as she role-played her character and helped solve the murder. She was really immersed in her "movie star" persona, which was an example for all of us would-be actors. The murderer was finally revealed, and our guilty friend smiled sheepishly and said how fun it was to have everyone trying to catch her. We all had a good time, but the night wasn't over yet. I had another event planned to keep the air of "mystery" going.

After dinner was over and the mystery was solved, we retired to the media room to watch the movie *Clue*. Based on the board game of the same name, what better film to cap the evening and keep the whodunit spirit alive, right? The suspense of the game and the movie was echoed within me as I wondered if my date wanted to elevate to the next level like I did. All signs pointed to "yes" as I quickly reminisced all the dates and activities that we enjoyed together. When arranging seats for the movie, however, the suspense in my mind built up and ended in disappointment. She sat at the far end of the sofa with her arms folded throughout the movie. Not a good sign, and foreshadowed the truth of her feelings.

Two days later I found out from her that she didn't want a boyfriend. Then another friend of mine said that he'd talked to her where she admitted that she liked hanging out with me, but only wanted to be friends. As disappointing as that was, because she was a great girl, I remember the evening fondly and still consider it a successful evening. Everyone had fun, and that's the point after all, isn't it?

Recipe:

Barbecue Shredded Pork Sandwiches

You'll need a crock-pot.

- 2 pork roasts
- 2 bottles of barbeque sauce (your choice in flavor)
- Fresh garlic cloves
- Hamburger buns (enough for 16 sandwiches)

Makes about 16 sandwiches (depending on the amount of pork per sandwich)

This recipe is really easy. First, take the pork roasts and make sure they're drained, then put them in a crock-pot. Cut slits in them and put pieces of garlic inside. Cook the meat on low to medium for at least 5 to 6 hours. When the meat is done, drain it from its juices and shred with a fork. Next, add the barbecue sauce. Voila— you have a tasty meal with little effort.

Creative Date #24

Progressive Dinner

The progressive dinner is a lot of fun, but can wind up being expensive, depending on where you go. I actually heard about this idea while in college. The main draw about this is the opportunity to visit different restaurants and sample something at each. You won't have a whole meal at each place, which might seem odd, but is actually pretty cool. This date is designed for a group, but can also be fun with just you and another person.

To prepare for this, you'll need to think of several different restaurants you and your date might like to visit. Then you write them down on pieces of paper, and put those little pieces in your hat, or a bowl, or whatever you want, really. One of you picks the first paper, and whatever that restaurant is will be the spot for appetizers. Afterwards, pick again, and head on over to that restaurant for the main course. Then pick one more time for the dessert.

To make it even more creative, you can think up a little riddle that disguises the name of the restaurant. For example, for *The Olive Garden*, you might write something like this: "Popeye's girlfriend probably enjoys eating at this Italian Restaurant." You don't want to make it so abstract that people can't figure it out, but you'll also get points for creativity. Depending on the company, you can be as clever or as simple as you want.

What you need for this date:

You will need little pieces of paper and something to write down the restaurant names with, plus a container to put them in.

My experience with this date:

In college, I planned a group date with my two best buddies, John and Tim. We wanted it to be creative so we planned a progressive dinner. The girls didn't know what we were going to do; all they knew was that we told them not to eat dinner beforehand.

I went and picked up my date, Jackie, then met my roommates and their dates. We brought out the hat with the names of the restaurants and explained to the girls what we were going to do that evening. Intrigue and excitement filled their faces. The feeling of love bloomed in the air . . . okay, maybe I'm stretching the truth on that, but seriously, they were excited. They smiled and were eager to choose a place to go. The first we went to was a Mexican restaurant. The chips and salsa were really good, and appetizers just as tasty. We even had a guy come around with his guitar and play us music for some authentic ambiance.

The next paper was chosen and we went to a barbecue joint. We got messy eating ribs and Jackie and I bonded over cornbread. Exactly what I imagined true love to be, of course. The last place was an ice cream parlor, where I shared a nice bowl of bubblegum ice cream with my date.

Even though we didn't work out in the long run, our progressive dinner was unique and memorable enough to stick with me forever.

Creative Date #25

Progressive Date

The progressive date follows a similar format as the progressive dinner, except that instead of restaurants, you'll pick activities out of a hat. The actual dates themselves don't necessarily have to be creative, but the very act of putting them in the hat makes it a fun and exciting event, and somewhat of a mystery. Some ideas you can put in the hat are mini-golfing, indoor rock climbing, video games, or bowling, among many other things.

What you need for this date:

Just like the progressive dinner, all you need are some ideas and something to write them down on, as well as something to put them in.

My experience with this date:

One time, my friend Jack and I wanted to do a double date that was exciting, and something new we hadn't done before. We wanted the girls to have a lot of fun as well, so I came up with the progressive date idea.

We picked the girls up and explained to them the idea for the date. I don't mean to brag, but they were really excited. I even received

Creative Date #26

Culinary Collaboration, Anyone?

This one really doesn't need very much of an explanation. When it comes to food, you don't have to spend all your money on some fancy restaurant. Making dinner with your date is a great way to impress them and score some major points.

Being together in this kind of setting gives you time to talk, get to know each other, and all the stuff in between—you know, like "accidentally" bumping into them. Pass the spatula, you ask? Well, sure I can, and I may or may not tickle you in the side as I hand it to you. Smooth, I tell you. Smooth as a good Béarnaise sauce.

It really doesn't matter what food you make. If you're in a group, it's fun to make something that everyone can help with. Something that I've done a couple of times in a group setting is Homemade Calzones. People, these are awesome. They're fun to make, don't cost a lot of money, and are delicious. It's a perfect opportunity to earn some brownie points by showing off your culinary skills, whether they're real or just faked for the night.

I grew up knowing how to cook. I cooked my first egg when I was only six years old. I remember accidentally breaking the yoke and, since I love them sunny side up, I was pretty upset by it. Mom stepped in and that's when I learned how to crack an egg with precision. Thanks, Mom. She taught me how to cook and I will always give her the credit for my skills in the kitchen.

I love cooking so much that a few years ago, I actually started a cooking channel on YouTube called, *In the Kitchen with Matt*. I wanted to be able to cook "with" other people, if you will, even if it was just a virtual setting, which leads me back to the date idea. As mentioned before, Calzones are good to make because they're easy and everyone gets involved, but this is your date, so make whatever you like, just make sure everyone can play a part in crafting the meal for the evening.

What you need for this date:

It really depends on what you are going to make. If you would like to make Calzones, watch the video here, or use the following recipe:

Mini Sausage Calzones

From *In the Kitchen with Matt*

Ingredients:

- 1 package frozen bread dough, thawed
- 1 package sweet Italian sausage about a half a pound
- 1 chopped onion
- 1 to 2 cloves garlic minced
- 1 teaspoon dried basil
- 1 teaspoon dried oregano
- 1 to 2 small 4 ounce cans of Italian style tomato sauce (depends on how saucy you want the inside)
- 1 bag of shredded mozzarella cheese (the more the merrier)

- Grated Parmesan cheese
- 1 egg
- Some milk

Makes enough for about 8 people

1. Divide dough into a bunch of portions. In your frying pan add your sausage and using your pancake turner/spatula cut it up into little pieces it will look similar to ground beef by this point. Add the onions and garlic and grill for a bit longer. Preheat oven to 425, grease baking sheet.

2. Add in basil, oregano and tomato sauce into skillet; turn down the heat and let it simmer for a bit longer, usually about 10 minutes. Roll each dough piece into a circle as big as you want it. Put sausage mixture onto each circle; pile on the cheese.

3. Add water to the edges of the dough. Fold dough over to make your calzone. Place on prepared baking sheet.

4. In another bowl put the egg and milk in it and beat it. Brush over Calzones. Bake for about 15 minutes or until golden brown. Serve immediately. You may also freeze uncooked Calzones and cook them at a later date.

My experience with this date:

I have yet to make dinner with someone and not liked it. It doesn't cost that much to cook a really nice meal, and everyone has fun doing it.

The last time I did this date idea, it was really successful and everyone helped out. Everyone talked with each other and asked some get-to-know questions. The food was incredible. I think the calzones get better every time I make them. We tried making an apple desert calzone and it didn't turn out right, but it wasn't a complete fail, because the experience was worth it.

After eating we went and played Laser Tag. My date, Michelle, was pretty handy with a gun. Good thing she was on my team. We won the game and afterwards, at the request of the girls, stopped at the gas station mini-mart for soft-freeze ice cream. I made dinner another time for Michelle on a solo date, and as you can guess, I was pretty interested in her. I surprised myself with that meal by cooking semi-authentic Filipino food, which was to die for, along with exquisite sautéed shrimp. For dessert we had strawberries on top of sliced Mango.

While cooking the dinner, just the two of us, we talked about a lot of things, she hinted at going out again, which I of course liked.

After the evening, I walked her home. She gave me a smile and nice long tight hug before going inside. But alas, it looks like I may have read her blatantly obvious signals wrong, as it wasn't meant to be. Some girls are easy to read, and others are so nice that you haven't got a clue. I guess it would all be much simpler if I had the power to read women's minds like Mel Gibson had in the movie *What Women Want*. Well, maybe it wouldn't be *that* great. I could hear a lot of things that I might rather not want to know.

Creative Date #27

Get all Up in That Mountain Grill

For the nature enthusiasts, going up to a mountain park and barbecuing tasty meats is a fun idea. One of my favorite things to do on this group date is make shish kabobs. To liven it up, barbecue the shish kabobs in a park, then sit down afterwards and watch a movie on a laptop or play night games. Parks in the mountains make the best get-away, but even the neighborhood park will do as a last resort.

What you need for this date:

This date is quite simple. You need to bring blankets, any snacks to go with the barbecue, a laptop (with extra batteries), and Frisbees, footballs, etc. Obviously, all the ingredients you'll use for the barbequed meat is necessary, and don't forget the small things like spices and skewers. You'll need a park that has grilling accommodations, or you could bring your own grill.

For a great dish, you can see the video I have for the kabobs on my cooking show.

Shish Kabob Recipe

I make it different every time but these are the main ingredients that I use.

- Shish Kabob Skewers
- Red Bell Peppers
- Green Bell Peppers (the mildest)
- Orange Peppers
- Pineapple (fresh works and tastes the best, but canned works fine too) Save Juice.
- Cherry tomatoes
- Sirloin steak cut in small bite-sized pieces
- Kielbasa sausage cut in bite-sized pieces
- Mushrooms (buy the ones that are already cut)

You can add almost anything you want to the kabob. The above ingredients are my favorite ones to use. Make sure everything is cut into bite-sized pieces; usually a little bigger than a quarter. Set them aside as you make the sauce, or you can have someone else put them on the skewers while you work.

The sauce is the key to making a delicious kabob.

- Pineapple juice (I usually use what is left over from the can of chunks or buy some)
- Soy sauce (about ¾ cup)
- ½ cup of brown sugar

- ½ cup of white wine vinegar or balsamic vinegar (you can use normal vinegar too)
- 1 Tsp. crushed red pepper
- 1 Tsp. ginger

Combine all of the above ingredients in a small saucepan. On low heat, bring the mixture to a boil and let bubble for two minutes. Put sauce aside.

Take the kabobs and grill them. Make sure to turn them about every 3-4 minutes. The kabobs usually take 10 to 15 minutes to cook, sometimes faster, depending on the heat from the barbeque. When the kabob is done dip it in the sauce. ENJOY!!!

My experience with this date:

It was a dark and stormy night. The road was slick from the pelting rain; our car slid several times, each time a bit closer to the edge of the road, with a five hundred foot cliff to its side. No doubt the railing wouldn't hold if we crashed into it. My date squeezed my arm in terror as we wound our way up the narrow mountain pass. Lightening, then thunder, then more rain . . . it was terrifying. Okay, I'm joking; I just always wanted to start a story that way.

I've made the shish kabobs numerous times for group barbecues, however one summer I had the opportunity to do it as a group date. The girl I asked out, Kelsey, was someone I met while playing volleyball with some of my friends. She actually had just moved in with a few girls that I knew and seemed like a fun girl to get to know, so I asked her out.

I wanted a buddy of mine, Dave, to come along, but he was visiting from out of town so I had to find a date for him, which wasn't a problem.

This is where things get interesting. First, my friend took forever to get ready. Seriously Dave, don't you know that rule number one in dating is, don't be late? So we didn't wind up picking our dates up until 20 minutes after we told them. They didn't say anything, but I could see Kelsey peering at me, eyes narrowed, as if looking into my soul and asking, *how could you be late, Matt? How??* Or maybe she was just thinking about how great I looked that evening. Could've been either.

Kelsey looked really good, beyond good, breathtaking even. Finally, we started driving up the canyon to where the park in the mountains was. I planned it so Kelsey and I would be in my car alone. Dave and his date drove up with another friend, Mike, and his date. As we were driving, Kelsey told me that she really doesn't like camping or outdoorsy stuff. Oops. I told her that she would like this date. We get there and it's dark already, thanks to Dave and his tardiness. Not to mention it's frigid. Kelsey then mentions that she also really hates the cold. Oops again. Eventually, we get everything ready and start to make the kabobs, and I find out Kelsey doesn't like most of the ingredients that go on them. Oops a million times over. As the bitter air chilled our bones, the gas for the grill we brought ran out. Oops, oops, and oops forever. But since Dave and I are big strong men, we didn't panic; we improvised and used wood instead.

After we were done eating, we decided that it might be too cold to watch a movie in the park like we'd planned, so we decided to go back to Mike's house to watch the movie. Just to add more disaster to the date, the only movies that we had with us were ones Kelsey had already seen a bunch of times, not to mention that while we were watching it, Mike's cat kept snooping around the group. And guess what? Kelsey is allergic to cats. She sniffled and sneezed the whole time during the movie. Yikes.

I still had fun on the date, and even though Kelsey said she had a good time, I'm not so sure that she did. But it was okay; her and I didn't connect, otherwise I would have asked her out again. Moral of the story: a little research goes a long way, and oh yeah, don't be late! And just in case you've forgotten one of the most important parts of a date, here's a reminder: don't forget to bring treats.

Creative Date #28

Three-Legged Ultimate Frisbee

Have you ever played Ultimate Frisbee? Well, for a twist on the game, get a big group together and play it three-legged.

Make sure you pick someone that you don't mind being attached to for the duration of the game, as you'll be quite close. This is a good date that blends humor with athletics, and is pretty funny to see couples falling over as they go for the Frisbee. This is completely free, as long as you have things around the house you can use as ties. You can play it in a park or on a school field, or anywhere with a large amount of grass. I don't recommend playing it on cement, unless you're yearning for a bloody nose. Basically, it's almost guaranteed that you'll fall over at some point in the game.

What you need for this date:

It's simple; all you need is a large group, a place to play, and some ties, the softer the better. You also need the most important item: a Frisbee, or a disc, as hard-core Ultimate Frisbee players will call it.

My experience with this date:

Several years ago, a large group of us got together and did a date. We didn't want to spend a lot of money so we picked something that would be really fun but cheap. Three-legged ultimate Frisbee was my choice, and after I told everyone how it was done, they thought it would be awesome. It was sort of a blind date, in a way, where all the guys' names are in a hat and all the girls' names are in another hat. The names were drawn and a guy was paired up with a girl. If it were a total mismatch, like a 5'10 girl with a 5'3 guy, we would change it by putting one of the names back and drawing again until at least the heights matched.

We got our dates and went to a sandwich place first for lunch. My date was a girl that was cool, but I didn't have any interest in her. It was still fun eating lunch and chatting with the group, though. After lunch we headed to the park. To make it totally free, you can skip the lunch part. At the park, we got out the ties, divided the couples into teams and began. It was hilarious watching as couples tripped over each, banged shoulders, and just stumbled all over the place. It was a blast, but my ankle got terribly sore because I got stuck with the worst of the ties. Remember how I said to bring soft ties? Listen to that advice.

Overall, everyone that came enjoyed the experience. Dating success!

Creative Date #29

Decathlon or Die

Time for some sports. The idea behind this date is to have a whole day of athletic activities planned so that you not only get a good workout, you get to spend a lot of time together as well.

You can plan this with a group of friends, which is great if you're playing something that needs more people. The events are up to you, but the point is to do several sports in one date. You might want to start at the climbing gym, then head to the sand volleyball courts or the beach for some volleyball, then over to the park to play ultimate Frisbee, or Frisbee golf. Speaking of golf, you can then go to a mini-golf place, then at the end of the day head to a pool and swim, play water polo, or just relax in the hot tub.

It's really up to you how you plan the events. It would be good to plan sports that are a little different from each other so you're not always running—a good mix will allow you to make a whole day of it. Also, make sure to allow time for food breaks. Don't want your date to get "hangry," do you?

Make it even more interesting by planning weird sports instead of the conventional ones. Instead of football do foosball; instead of volleyball do Wally ball; instead of mini-golf, play botchy ball.

What you need for this date:

This one is easy to figure out—if you are going to play football, make sure to have a football, and so on. Put everything in your trunk for easy access during the day.

My commentary on this date:

The decathlon date is something I thought up while in the process of writing this book. I thought to myself, "What kinds of things do I enjoy doing?" I then rattled off a bunch of activities that were sports related, put them together and called it a decathlon date. Pretty creative, eh?

The trick to an incredibly successful, tremendously delightful date is to pick someone that likes all of the sports you're going to play. Maybe you can be sneaky and do your homework beforehand to find out what kind of sports they like, or use some get-to-know you questions to get your answer. You can do this kind of date with your spouse, as well; in which case you probably already know what kind of sports to plan.

The number of sports you do in one date isn't the most important thing; it can be ten, or it can be two. What's big is who you're with and how much fun you have.

Recently, I drove about an hour-and-a-half one way to meet a girl whom I had been conversing with online. We met for lunch and then went and played tennis. She actually was a collegiate tennis player and . . . let's just say I got my butt kicked. After, we played another game right there on the tennis court, and again, got my butt kicked. While it wasn't exactly a decathlon and was only two activities, it was quite the workout. Such a fun date—I texted her a few days later to see if she wanted to go out again, but it turns out she'd decided to start dating someone else exclusively.

Creative Date #30

Get Your Extreme Sports On

There are places you can go that have all kinds of extreme sports to do.

A place I used to live by was called Extreme Sports Center. This place had fun and unique activities like padded suit sumo wrestling, gladiator fighting, laser tag, obstacle courses, and video games. It was perfect; if you and your date are in a competitive mood, grab a group of friends and go to a place like this and have at it. These types of places are usually not very expensive either, so it won't break your budget. This makes a really fun group date activity, or you can even do it with just the two of you. Some other related places are trampoline parks; one near where I live now is called "Jumpstreet." It is basically a warehouse with a ton of different trampolines to play on.

What you need for this date:

Search for a place like this online near you and then show up and be dressed for the occasion.

My commentary on this date:

A few years ago, we got together a big group of people with a nice mix of men and women. We weren't paired up, so it wasn't really a "date," per se, but was fun just the same. We went to a place called "Extreme Fun Center" to test our skills against each other. It was super funny watching my friends get dressed up in the sumo outfits and wrestle with each other, and also play in the big obstacle course that kind of looked like something that would be at a McDonalds playland, only bigger. A big attraction there was a harness that you put on which was connected to a bungee cord; you were supposed to run as far as you could without getting pulled back. I didn't get that far. The Gladiator arena was cool, too; people were falling over left and right.

The best part? I didn't see one person without a smile on their face.

Creative Date #31

Start Your Engines!

For some reason, small motor vehicles are entertaining to adults and not just kids. You would think that driving your much bigger and more powerful car would be enough fun for you, but no, go-karts are where it's at. I think adults like go-karts because it allows them to be young again; kids like them because they get to drive and feel like adults. This is fun for all ages, whether you are taking your kids for a ride, want to do it alone, or do it on a date.

Unless you own your own go-kart, you'll probably want to plan something else after you're done riding, as the races don't usually last that long. You may find a location that not only offers go-kart racing, but also has other games that you can play, like a fun center for example.

What you need for this date:

All you need to do is look online to see where the nearest go-karting place is and make sure it's open when you want to go.

My experience with this date:

I've gone go-karting several times. A few years ago, I took a girl to a fun center that had a driving range, an arcade, and go-karts. We went to the driving range first, where I showed her how to hit a golf ball, and then we tested our mad go-kart skills on the track. The kids we raced on the track didn't know what hit them. Alright, fine. I'm pretty sure we both lost to them. But the date was so much fun, all the same.

Creative Date #32

Add-on Storytelling

An add-on story starts with you giving everyone in the group a sheet of paper and a pencil or pen.

Everyone begins writing a story, then after a minute or two, you fold the paper over until only the last line of the story can be read, and pass it to the person on your right. Each person reads the last line of the new story in front of them and continues the story for another block of time until folding and passing to their right. This continues until you get yours back. When it comes time for everyone to write the very last segment of the story in front of them, they should end it. After all has been written, each person stands up in turn and reads their story. It's pretty funny what kinds of ideas develop from this. Most don't make sense at all, which only makes it more hilarious.

This date is totally free, so it works great for groups of people on tight budgets. And the more the merrier when it comes to this activity; small groups don't give you nearly the laughs as a larger one.

What you need for this date:

You need enough paper for each person, plus writing utensils. That's it. And of course, treats to eat afterwards.

My commentary on this date:

When I was a young whippersnapper, my older brother introduced me to this activity. We happened to be having a family gathering and wanted to play some sort of game, so he suggested Add-on Storytelling. There were about 7 of us, so the size was pretty good for the activity. I really liked the game as a twelve-year-old, but when I actually developed writing skills and a love for writing is when I fully appreciated the game and how it can be used to create fun memories. This is a great activity for a group date, especially if you want your date laughing. People like to laugh, so why not give them the opportunity?

Several years ago, a large group of us were over at a friend's house for games. I suggested this and we all played it. The best part was when everyone took turns reading his or her's finished story out loud. Hilarious. This was not a group date, per se; it was just a bunch of girls and guys that got together for a fun evening. And it was fun, no doubt—afterwards, we even ate some amazing homemade chocolate chip cookies that I had baked.

Creative Date #33

Lights, Camera, Action!

A really entertaining group date idea is to get together and make a movie. You can have one person write the script or all participate in writing it, then film it with a video camera or your smart phone. These home movies usually turn out really funny and are something you can keep and share with your family.

If you have a digital video camera you can edit the movie on your computer, then burn it onto a DVD/Blu-Ray or just upload the file to YouTube. These days, the camera on your phone will work well if you don't have access to a video camera. This can be a totally free date, assuming you have the equipment, not to mention something really fun to do!

What you need for this date:

To make this date happen you need people to both be in the movie and work the camera, and you'll need a story to tell, usually in the form of a script. The script doesn't have to be fancy; it could be just scribbled on a piece of paper, really. No elaborate Hollywood formats needed. For recording, you'll want either a digital video camera or a good smart phone, and then a computer program to edit with like iMovie.

My commentary on this date:

I have always made movies since I was younger; in fact, video production has been my career for the past several years. In college, my roommates and I wanted to make a movie, and since video production was my major, I took it upon myself to write the short script. We invited some girls over to make the movie with us, and got started. It was a quite amusing, hilarious even, although I might have gotten upset a few times when my good friend kept looking right into the camera, which is a big no-no in the movie making world.

The home video was basically a cheesy "Slasher" film about a guy in a Marvin the Martian mask going around killing college students. It took us about four hours that evening to film the short eight-page script. The next week I was able to edit it on the computer, and then we had a party while we watched it. Now several years later, every time I see it, the fond memories of that evening come pouring in.

One of the girls in the movie actually married one of my best friends, who was my roommate at the time, too. I seemed to do that a lot—taking girls out that my friends or acquaintances ended up marrying. Some guys even started the slogan that if "A guy wants a girl, just have Matt take her out first." Still not totally sure what it means, but it's pretty funny.

Creative Date #34

Where's Waldo

Another fun free group date activity is playing *Where's Waldo* in the mall. What you do is have one of the couples dress up without you knowing what they'll be, then go to the mall and walk around, shop, etc. They'll try their hardest to blend in and hide in plain sight. Then, all the other couples in the group have to search the mall and find them. This type of thing can be as fun as you make it, and works really well for people who like to dress up and play different characters. When you're done, you can all gather at the food court and grab a treat or something else to eat.

What you need for this date:

You need costumes for the couple that will be disguised. Preferably you just tell them in advance to dress up and go to the agreed upon location, then get straight to finding them.

My commentary on this date:

When I was a teenager I first played this game as a big group, and we had tons of fun. Once again there was a girl there that I liked, and she happened to be someone that I had had a crush on for probably four years, but nothing ever came of it. Fast forward to a handful of years ago when I suggested this date to a group. We played, we laughed, we all had the best time.

Creative Date #35

Spin the Bottle

Say whaaat? Spin the bottle? Why yes, it's that game. You know, the one you secretly wished to be able to play when you were thirteen, the one that may have given you your first awkward kiss.

For a hilarious time and a bit of nostalgia, you could play spin the bottle with your group. This date works well if you are at least somewhat attracted to the girls/guys in the group; it's also great if you haven't kissed anyone in a long time, because dang it, sometimes you just need a kiss. As a bonus, if you learn the proper technique on how to spin the bottle then you can get it to land wherever you want, meaning you can kiss exactly who you want. Kind of sneaky, I know, but hey, gotta do what you can if you want to kiss the girl. "There you see her, sitting there across the way, you don't got a lot to say, but you're dying to spin the bottle, because you want to kiss the girl . . ." Okay, that is a cheesy song about spin the bottle that sounds exactly like the song from *Little Mermaid*. How do I know that song, you ask? Because that is one of my favorite Disney movies of all time, and I had a crush on Ariel when I was a kid. No judgments, please—redheads are hot.

What you need for this date:

You just need a bottle and a place to play.

My experience with this date:

I've played this game a bunch of times on group dates. My friends and I coordinated each other's dates so that we'd be attracted to all girls involved, for obvious reasons. One time, I was able to kiss my friend's date (who happened to be extremely good looking) like five times. My date kissed me probably only three times. It was hilarious. Did I mention I was only twelve years old? All right, spin the bottle is meant more to be funny and not a real date to be taken seriously. I guess you really could play this game, but just a warning—everyone will probably laugh at you when you bring it up. In reality, though, adults need fun like this at times, and if for some reason you do decide to play this game, you probably shouldn't bring dates, just get a big group of fun guys and girls together who don't mind this kind of activity.

Creative Date #36

Yeehaw, It's Rodeo Time

Rodeos are very entertaining; you get to see barrel raises, bull riding, calf roping, etc. Everyone is dressed up like a cowboy or cowgirl—it's a lot of fun. Rodeos usually aren't expensive to attend, either and usually cost a little more than a full-priced movie. If your date is a big country fan, surprise them by going to the rodeo.

What you need for this date:

It is pretty easy to find out where the nearest rodeo is going to be by looking online. If you happen to live in another country and are reading this book, maybe find an activity that would be similar.

My experience with this date:

I had the opportunity to go to my first rodeo one summer. There were a couple of girls that lived in our apartment complex, and they just "happened" to have extra tickets, so they invited us to go with them. I had my reservations about this whole rodeo idea, but since it was going to be free and I had nothing better to do, I decided to go.

We arrived near the rodeo and had to park about a quarter of a mile away because the parking lot was super packed. My spirits lifted when I saw all sorts of cute girls walking around. I couldn't believe it was my first time coming to one of these. We found our seats and the rodeo began. I had a blast. I didn't think it would be that fun, but it was extremely entertaining. I think the coolest thing was when they were bull riding, and also at the end of the rodeo they had motocross guys jumping in the air doing tricks.

Then it started raining. That wasn't really fun. I'm kind of like a cat: I hate the rain. But all in all, the rain didn't spoil the overall fun, and I ultimately got a night out with cute girls, outside and loving it. Not a bad way to spend the evening.

Creative Date #37

Board Game Night

One thing I love to do is play board games, from *Settlers of Catan,* to *7 Wonders,* to *Dominion,* along with some of the classics like *Monopoly* or *Risk.* If your date happens to like board games, it makes for a great group date activity. Game nights are bound to have lots of laughs, friendly banter, and a chance to show off some gaming skills, trivia knowledge, or *Pictionary* prowess—it all depends on what you play. I have a group of friends that I regularly play with; we always wind up having a great night, although sometimes it can get pretty competitive!

What you need for this date:

   You need some awesome board games to play, a place to play them, probably some snacks, and you guessed it, treats.

My experience with this date:

   A few years ago one of my best friends, Gabe, invited me over to his house for a board game date night. Him and his wife had a blind date lined up for me. I am no stranger to blind dates, and am generally okay with the idea of getting set up with someone I don't know, especially in a low-pressure environment like a game night. The evening was fun; we played a cooperative board game called *Robinson Crusoe,* which had us all on the same team trying to beat the board. Co-op games, as they are called, are especially good if you want the competitive spirit to be wrangled in. My date was attractive (well done, Gabe, on the set-up), but we really didn't connect that well. At least that's how it was for me, which is a shame because I found out from Gabe that she wanted me to ask her out afterwards.

Creative Date #38

Hell's Kitchen

Bring out the competitive spirit and put your culinary skills to the test by having a cook-off with your group. One couple can be the judge while the rest create a main course, or maybe you can all vote on which one is the best. Then afterwards, you'll of course have a ton of fun eating all the food.

Knowing how to cook, and cook well, is quite the impressive skill to have. Ladies love it, men love it—you can't go wrong with showing off cooking talents. You could do it with any idea, whether it is a main dish, or a desert, or an appetizer. The important thing is to have a fun time cooking with your date; winning the competition comes in second. A close second. It's up to you what the prize for the winner will be.

What you need for this date:

You need all the ingredients for whatever dish you are going to make. To keep it fair for each couple, you should set a limit on how much you can spend on the ingredients. Make them come up with something delicious for only $5 or $10, or whatever amount you decide. This will definitely test your creativity with food. You could all meet at one place before setting the rules, then go to the store and get the stuff, take it back to your individual places and cook it, then all meet back at one place and have the judging and eating party. You may, depending on the size of the kitchen, all be able to cook at the same location, but again, that will depend on the size of the kitchen, how many burners and ovens there are, etc. Maybe even set it up like the show *Chopped* and list 4 different ingredients that each couple have to use in their dish. On my YouTube channel, *In the Kitchen with Matt,* you might find some good ideas.

My commentary on this date:

I have never competed in a cook-off but I think it would be a really fun thing to do, especially in a date setting. Watch out, Iron Chef! With that said, I have been to plenty of potlucks where there was most certainly a secret competition to see who brought the best food.

Creative Date #39

Find Your Date

I am a huge fan of treasure hunting and scavenger hunt activities, so I thought up this group date to go along with my love of adventure.

The date basically entails clues being dropped off at the dates' houses. It helps if they know each other so that they can communicate well and search together. And what are they searching for? That's right—this is a treasure hunt for you. They'll get a clue, which leads to another clue. The first one might have them "go and look under the nearest big M." Then they go to McDonalds and find the next clue, etc. It is up to you how many twists and turns you send them on. It would also be funny to borrow a car that they won't recognize, follow them around and watch as they try and put the clues together that will lead them to you.

The tricky part is coming up with the clues. You want them creative but not hard to understand; fun but not too over the top. It's not always easy to think of them but I'm sure you can think up something good. When you get to the end of the date, have dinner together and do something fun afterwards.

You could make it more interesting by having it be a blind date for one of the couples. That way she/he is anticipating the whole time who their date is going to be at the end. Intrigue is always a good night.

What you need for this date:

In order to make this date really fun you will have to think up clues. They can be little notes of paper with riddles on them that lead to the next clue. If the dates know each other, have them all meet at one of their houses, and that way you can leave the first note at their door. Maybe you can doorbell ditch them and then get out of sight, and when they leave, follow behind to the first clue. There's a bunch of different ways you could do it, but just be sure to have something planned at the end. Make it pretty cool, too, because your date might get a little upset if after they reach the end of the clues you say, "Good job on finding us—time to take you home."

My commentary on this date:

This is similar to a scavenger hunt, only for this you aren't looking for objects, unless of course your date happens to be the object of your affection. This is something exciting, something new, and something sure to impress.

Creative Date #40

Truth or Dare Jenga

Relive childhood memories by playing truth or dare Jenga on a group date activity. This is great for a first date, but also fun for couples that have been together for a long time.

In case you didn't already know, Jenga is a game where you have little rectangular blocks stacked up into a tower, and the object is to pull out individual blocks without letting the tower fall. Truth or dare Jenga is the same idea, but there are truths and dares written on the blocks of wood. If the pile falls down, the person responsible will have to do the ultimate dare. The game is usually inexpensive to buy or you can just borrow it from someone. I know it sounds childish but hey, it is really a lot of fun.

What you need for this date:

You can buy Truth or Dare Jenga at any store that sells board games. That is the only expense that you will need. If you already have the game or can borrow it, then it'll be totally free.

My experience with this date:

My friend, Jason, and I were both set up on a blind date by a mutual friend of ours. We wanted to do something fun that wouldn't cost a ton of money, being poor college students at the time. So we decided on making dinner together and playing Truth or Dare Jenga. We invited my engaged friends to participate in our date as well to make it three couples. Our dates lived together, so Jason and I drove to their house and picked them up. My first impression was a good one; she was pretty hot. I'd have to see how the night went . . .

We made homemade calzones for dinner; everyone participated, which made the dinner making a lot more fun. The conversation was genuine, no uncomfortable pauses or anything like that. After dinner we played the game. It was awesome. The ultimate dare, which wasn't really bad at all, was for my friend's fiancée. She had to stand on the balcony of our apartment complex and scream at the top of her lungs, "I love you, Jim!" I think she got off pretty easy. The date went well, the food was excellent, and the game was enjoyable. And even though I didn't end up going out for a second time with my date, it still wasn't a terrible setup by any means.

Creative Date #41

Fondue Party

Another food date, which is great for a group setting, is a Fondue party. Fondue is basically a type of dip in which you dip fruit, meat, vegetables, or crackers in. Depending on the food you use, it can be very delicious.

An example is chocolate fondue with strawberries and other fruits. Who doesn't like taking a giant ripe strawberry and dipping it into silky smooth warm chocolate? Heaven on earth, I tell you. This date allows for very good conversation, a place to tell stories, reminisce, or just relax and eat good food. After eating, do something fun: board games, add-on storytelling, etc.

What you need for this date:

You need the recipe and all the ingredients, which is pretty simple. Basically, you get some chocolate candy wafers and melt them until smooth. If you happen to have a chocolate fountain or know someone who has one, that is a bonus—those things are awesome. You also need the food that will be dipped in the fondue, like different kinds of fruit, for example. Step it up a notch by decorating the table with a nice tablecloth, good china, centerpiece, candles, etc.

My experience with this date:

Several years ago for dinner one summer evening, my sister in-law made fondue for all of us. My friend was over as well, but she was just a friend. Yes, it's perfectly okay to have a date with a friend without any further expectations of having another date; just two good friends getting together for an enjoyable time.

The food was scrumptious. We had a milk chocolate fondue, as well as a marshmallow cream fondue and cheese fondue. We had a variety of fruits that we dipped in the chocolate and marshmallow, and then a spread of crackers and meats that we dipped in the cheese. The conversation flowed as we chatted about various things from movies to sports, and even told some stories from the past. The evening was an excellent one.

Creative Date #42

Frisbee Golf

A great group date idea that blends athletics with conversation and fresh air is Frisbee golf, otherwise known as Disc golf, which is the proper term for it.

Frisbee golf can be played on the beach or basically anywhere that has open space. There are actually parks out there that have a legitimate Disc Golf course, which consists of Metal Baskets that serve as targets. You can also just set up cones and try to hit them with your Frisbee.

First, you set up the course by putting the cones or objects in different locations around the park or beach. If you lucked out and are playing on an actual disc golf course, then you won't need to set anything up, you will just need your discs. Next, you have a starting point where you will throw the Frisbee. The object of the game is to hit the obstacles in as few throws as possible. You throw the Frisbee and if it doesn't hit the first time, then you pick it up where it landed and try again, setting up the course so that the distances vary from long to short. If played in a group date scenario you could compete as teams. Maybe you could mix it up for each hole, too, like on one hole you have to both hold and throw the Frisbee, the next hole, maybe you have to throw it between your legs or over your head, etc. Have fun with it.

What you need for this date:

You need a Frisbee and cones or objects to use as the "holes," an open location to play in, or you need to find a disc golf course and bring the special discs, which you can buy online or at places like Big 5 Sporting Goods. This date is really cheap, maybe even free if you already have the equipment, and is fun for the whole group.

My experience with this date:

I have played Frisbee golf and Disc golf a bunch of times, on the beach and in the park, with big groups. After dinner one evening, I took my date to the park and we played some disc golf. She had never heard of the game, but since she liked playing miniature golf and ultimate Frisbee she was intrigued when I described the game to her. We had a blast searching out our targets and letting the discs fly to their intended destinations, which can be a tricky feat at times. The disc doesn't always want to go the direction you want; sometimes it has a mind of its own and decides to curve the wrong way and land even further away than where you started. Yeah, good times, if that happens to your opponent. My date got a bit frustrated, but had loads of fun. She just needed a bit more practice, like most new things we try. It was a great first date activity. It gave us time to talk as well as have some friendly competition.

Creative Date #43

Disco Skating

Put on those bell-bottoms, grab your roller skates, and go back in time to the 70's where you spend the night at a roller rink disco skating.

Most of the roller rinks will have some kind of themed night each week, and usually they have a disco night. This is a great time to dress up with your date and do something wacky. If you both aren't really good at roller-skating then it should be pretty interesting. Part of the fun is dressing up in 70's garb. Even if they don't have a themed night, you can still dress up. Roller-skating is one of those dates that have lasted through the years, and can be done as a group or just as a couple.

What you need for this date:

Find a rink to skate at, get some disco clothes, and bring skates or rent them at the rink.

My commentary on this date:

I have gone Disco skating on several occasions, usually in large groups, where the girls are in plentiful supply. I was not blessed with agility and good balance when it comes to strapping moveable objects on my feet. However, I take pride in the fact that I haven't fallen while roller-skating since I was a kid, knock on wood. Truthfully, I never fall because even a tortoise would be able to beat my pace on the rink. Yeah, I'm old and would rather go slow than wind up breaking something. But even if I do skate like I'm 90 years old, I still have a good experience each time I go.

Creative Date #44

Top Golf

What is Top Golf? Top Golf is a driving range venue that is creeping up all over the United States. It is pretty much a driving range on steroids. Even if you have the worse golf swing in the world, you can still be competitive and may even win a game or two.

It's set up like a normal driving range, with major differences. The bays where you play feel more like bowling alley bays. If a driving range and a bowling alley had a baby, it would probably be Top Golf. What you'll do is reserve one of these bays, which hold several people, and even comes complete with all the golf clubs you'll need. Out in the field are several "holes" with flags and larger rings attached to it. Each ring has a different point system, similar to a dartboard. These holes, which are more like targets, just need a ball to roll or land in it to score points. Something great is the rings are large, making them fairly easy to hit.

To get an idea of the point system, the outer ring for a very close target might be worth 2 points, whereas the inner ring for that same close target is worth or 4 or 6 points. Then the further out the targets are, the more points they're worth. So take a golf ball, grab a club, and swing away exactly like you would at a driving range, except you'll aim for one of those targets. If you shank the ball, don't worry; chances are it might roll into another target, which will still score you points. Top Golf is an awesome place, great for a group date atmosphere. They also have a good selection of food that you can order, as well as Big Screen TVs so that you can watch the big game.

What you need for this date:

All you need for this date is to find out where the closest Top Golf location is to you. They have places all over the United States, as well as 3 locations in the United Kingdom, 1 coming soon in Australia, several coming soon to Canada, and 2 coming soon to Mexico. As of the publishing of this book, there are 33 scattered across the United States and about that same amount already announced or being built to add to that total. Visit their website for more details - https://topgolf.com/us/

My commentary on this date:

I have gone to Top Golf a few times now. Each time was with a big group, the first with my team from work, and the second was for a friend's birthday party. Everyone had a blast. While I personally have yet to take a date there, I know of plenty of people who have done that and loved it. Give it a shot if you've got one close by; you won't regret it.

Creative Date #45

Escape Room

An escape room is an adventure game where you and your team are confined to a physical location, and while inside you need to find, hints, clues, and secrets in order to "escape" the room.

These escape rooms are similar to situations that you might find yourself in while playing various video games on the market. You've also probably seen some horror or adventure movie at some point in your life where the main characters were stuck in some situation and they had to find a way to get out. Well, that's kind of like the escape room. Usually these games are set in a variety of "themed" locations. Maybe it is a medieval style room, set in the old west, or maybe something straight out of the Saw movies, or the Walking Dead, or maybe a science laboratory on a space station—you get the idea. This is a really good group date activity, or you could go as a couple and team up with a group to complete their team.

Grab your Sherlock Holmes sleuthing hat, get your adventure on and see if you can escape the room. Better yet, leave the hat at home.

What you need for this date:

Look online and find the closest escape room venue to you. They are located all over North America, Europe, Australia, New Zealand, East Asia, Russia, and South America. This is a good site for those living in the United States - https://roomescapeartist.com/find-a-room/

My commentary on this date:

This is something I have always wanted to do since I first heard about them. I have a friend who actually owns a couple of escape room venues. I have yet to experience this adventure firsthand, but have several friends who have participated in them with dates and loved it. Usually after escaping or not escaping the room, you take a group picture. Maybe you've even seen similar pictures of your friends on Facebook who've posted about their experiences escaping the room.

Chapter 3: Romantic Dates

"Just the Two of Us . . ." – For time alone with that special someone

It's time to get down to the nitty gritty, the brass tacks, the stuff that Valentine's Day dreams are made of. That's right, it's time to get your romance on.

Let's be honest, while group dates are fun, your relationship probably won't progress very far if you always have the safety net of a group. You need some alone time with your date, where you can truly get to know them. And if the situation arises, maybe a kiss—I know you want that kiss. This chapter will include all kinds of romantic ideas from the less expensive to the all-out wallet burning extravaganza that is sure to leave your date breathless.

Creative Date #46

The Push Her Over the Edge Tremendously Romantic Date

I call this date "The push her over the edge date," because I was going to use it on a girl that I liked a lot and I thought she really liked me as well, so I planned a date that would let her know how I felt while also finding out exactly how she felt.

The idea is this: you show up at your date's house, both of you dressed up classy (REMEMBER this date is not a first date. It is a romantic date that should be used with caution. It will work well with a spouse or significant other, and maybe also to push that special someone over the edge which hopefully—for you—will result in winding up with a significant other). Your date should know beforehand that you are taking her to a special restaurant that you think she will really like. Blindfold her and lead her to your car, then drive around until you get to your friend's house. You open the door and your friend is dressed up as a waiter, who then leads you to the balcony where a table is set up with candles and other romantic lighting. The sun is going down by this time.

Then remove the blindfold. There are cool little menus that you created beforehand laying on the table. On the menu is a special recipe, or a favorite dish, or maybe food from your date's favorite restaurant. If you like to cook then maybe the menu is a dish that you know how to make really well. Remember the atmosphere is what counts here, not necessarily the quality of the food, just as long as you know your date will like it. Have music playing in the background. If you prepared Italian food, make it Italian music, etc. This will help set the mood, especially before you take off the blindfold. By then, your date should think they are in a restaurant. You could even have background restaurant noises playing to further set the ambience and sell the restaurant atmosphere.

When your friend has finished serving you both dinner and dessert, have the music change to a favorite love song and slow dance on the balcony. When the sun is gone and the dancing is finished, retire to the family room and cuddle up and watch a romantic comedy together. Voila—a very fun, romantic, creative date.

What you need for this date:

You need a lot of things for this date. For one, you need a friend with a house or apartment that has a balcony and a great view. If not, improvise. Second, you need to prepare the menus, food, blindfold, flowers if you want them, table, music and whatever movie you are going to watch. There are a lot of details involved with this date and the more detail you have, the better it will be.

My commentary on this date:

I had the date all planned. My friend was actually going out of town that weekend and said that I could use his house, which had a balcony and an incredible view. I was going to have another friend come and be the waiter. The girl I'd been dating for a while, Jessica, came over and I played the date out magically. It was bliss, or so I thought.

We talked about going out, which she then replied that she couldn't go. Her tone of voice was off. I then asked her if I should keep asking her out. She said, "Under what pretenses?" Then I said something like, "Well, we have been going out for a while, yada, yada." She confessed that she didn't want a boyfriend, which basically meant she didn't want to date me anymore and just wanted to be friends. Ah, the good ole "F" word. I am still not quite sure what happened.

Creative Date #47

The Fantasy Date of a Lifetime

The bulk of this idea comes from the movies with a little mixture of my own creativity as well. This date idea is definitely for couples or spouses, and you will see why in a moment.

First, you need to have access to a lake where you can use a rowboat. Ideally, there is a floating platform out in the water, or maybe you could use a pier, which might be easier to locate. Even if you wind up using the pier, still use the boat to get to it instead of just walking. What you do is you pick up your date, tell her that you are going to a nice restaurant, and then take her to the lake. A blindfold on the way adds another level of suspense, but that's up to you.

After you arrive at the lake, you get into the boat and row your way out to the floating platform or the end of the wooden pier. Set up for you is a candlelight dinner. Bring a Bluetooth speaker and have music playing to paint the perfect mood. After you are finished eating, ask her to dance.

This next part is kinda tricky on how it will work: you need to have some kind of signal for your friend who is hiding on the shore. Once they see it, they'll launch off some bottle rockets (if legal where you are). In my mind, time the fireworks for when you go in and kiss your date, maybe while you're dancing.

Boom. Doesn't this sound like a movie? It'll take work and planning, but will be incredibly romantic. This would work well as a proposal date—you'd put all other fiancés to shame. Mark my words, if you recorded this proposal, it would go viral. And you don't have to follow these guidelines exactly; modify it as you choose to make it your own. Your date, spouse, or girlfriend will absolutely adore you for it, especially when they see all of the hard work and effort that was put into it.

What you need for this date:

There are a lot of things that you need for this date to work. You need a lake, a rowboat, a platform or pier, a table to set up for the dinner, and bottle rockets. You may not be able to get bottle rockets, but imagine the spectacle if you did. You will need a blindfold if you are planning to use one. You need the food that you will be eating, as well as a speaker for the mood music; the small ones that you can connect to your phone or ipod will work perfectly. You will need to have your friend hiding nearby where he can see well enough to launch off the bottle rockets at the right time. A video camera of some kind would be essential if you want to record the night as a keepsake.

Unlike the movies, where you can do multiple takes of a scene to get it right, you only get one chance at this date to do it right. But it's worth it. How do I know? Because I know everything, okay, in all seriousness, I've told a few girls about this date and they totally loved the idea; in fact, they almost melted right there.

My commentary on this date:

I just dreamed this date up one day. I was thinking about movies and romantic scenes in them. Then I started thinking about lakes and fireworks, put them all together with my candlelight dinner and dancing idea, and presto, the romantic date of the century. I will probably do this with the girl that I plan on marrying. I am not sure if I would use this date idea as my proposal date, but possibly. If the person you are in love with is fascinated with movies and sappy chick flicks and can't get enough romance in their life, do something like this date. It will take their breath away and leave you being the king/queen of romance.

Creative Date #48

Luxurious Dinner out at Sea

For a very romantic but expensive date, reserve a place on a yacht for dinner. Search for a marina that has dinner/lunch cruises, whether it's in the ocean or on a lake. Although they're usually pretty expensive, they're quite romantic.

After dinner, take her to the deck and dance in the moonlight. This is another one of those dates that you see in the movies, except that it doesn't have to be only done in the movies, it can actually be done in real life. One example of this is a dinner cruise in San Diego. I easily found this online. The cost ranged from $55 to $74 per adult. The cruise is a two-and-a-half-hour ride. This is only one example, but most cities on the coast will have a cruise like this available. There are even dinner cruises that happen on some of the major rivers and lakes in Canada and the United States, so if you don't happen to live near the ocean, check to see if there are dinner cruises close to you somewhere else. For example, Lake Tahoe has a twilight dinner cruise available. All you have to do is look around for one.

What you need for this date:

You definitely need to make reservations and show up on time for the cruise. That is all you need to do to prepare for this date. Make sure to dress up nicely, as well. This could be something that is done for an anniversary, a marriage proposal, or just because you want some extra brownie points.

My commentary on this date:

Many years ago, a good friend of mine went to a formal dance on a cruise ship in the San Francisco Bay Area. The city lights were exquisite, the ship was immaculate, and he said it was like being in a movie. Needless to say, his fiancée loved it. Doing something like this would be super romantic, although it might cost a pretty penny. Or maybe an ugly penny—I'm not sure how clean you keep your money.

Creative Date #49

Rooftop Dinner

Everyone knows that candlelight dinners are classic romantic dates. Or maybe you've lived in a cave and you have no idea what a hit they can be. But don't take my word for it . . . find out for yourself.

In order to make it a bit more interesting, set up a candlelight dinner on top of a roof. And don't risk death—it must be a flat roof, for obvious reasons. Depending on the location, this will be a very romantic date. You could even hire someone to play a musical instrument while you eat, like the violin, or have a friend come do it. Also make sure to have flowers for your date as a centerpiece that she can take home afterwards, and if you feel so inclined, dance with her under the stars—not too close to the edge, though!

What you need for this date:

You'll need a roof that you can do this on—a flat one. You'll find them on top of businesses and office buildings for the most part, although occasionally you'll find a home with it. The reason why this idea is cool is not just because of the awesome ambiance, but also because girls appreciate the time and effort that a guy has put into the date. So set up a table on the roof, and try and bring some lighting, like twinkling white lights. String them up for some added romance. Depending on the location, you can do this at sunset, or wait until dark.

My commentary on this date:

When I was a teenager, I would say around fourteen or fifteen, I came home from my friend's house and wanted to know where my older brother was. I asked my mom and she said that he was on the roof. I said okay, I thought maybe he was playing basketball and the ball got stuck up there, knowing, my parents' house has a flat roof. Anyways, I climbed up the ladder and there's my brother, setting up a candle light dinner for a girl that he liked. I thought he was weird. But of course I was naïve and she loved it. I can't remember if they ended up dating, but he didn't end up marrying her.

But even though that girl didn't work out for him, the date was still magical. My brother had a knack for coming up with creative romantic dates; some of my inspiration and ideas have come from him and his experiences.

Creative Date #50

Candle Light Dinner on Top of an Overpass

Yeah, I know, it's another candlelight dinner. So what? Can you blame me for being romantic? It's not my fault that candles add an irresistible glow to absolutely everything. I'd be doing dating a disservice if I didn't include candles in dates. Anyways, excuse my rant. Moving on . . .

A wonderfully creative place to set up a candlelight dinner is on top of an overpass. Hundreds of cars will pass underneath, allowing you to show the world that you aren't afraid if everyone knows how much you dig the person that you're with. Do it near sunset to heighten the romance. Make sure to have a friend dress up and be the waiter. You could buy the food or cook it yourself, depending on what your date likes. When creating a romantic dinner, always make sure you are making or buying food that you know your date will love. This is another one of those little things that lets them know you're paying attention to what they say. This date really should only be done with someone that likes you a lot or loves you; you could possibly use this as the "I like you more than a friend" date, but make sure it isn't your first date.

What you need for this date:

First, you need to find an overpass that has easy access so you can set up the table and food. Second, make sure there's good weather, as this date really doesn't work in the rain or snow. A nice sunset would work perfectly. Bring an mp3 player or use your phone so you can have mood music, as well. Have one of your friends be the waiter or waitress. It wouldn't hurt to blindfold your date as you lead her to your destination, either.

I am telling you, girls really like this type of thing. I was talking to a friend of mind and she said that girls really love flowers, creative dates, and other things that let them know the guy is thinking about them. The more effort you put in to being unique, the more it communicates you're different than just any other date out there.

My commentary one this date:

When I was a young lad, my second oldest brother did something truly spectacular, crazy, off the wall, and totally awesome for his girlfriend. He set up a candlelight dinner on one of the catwalk overpasses that you take on foot from one side of the freeway to the park on the other side. It was so cool. The only problem was that it was really windy that day, so the food quickly got cold.

But it was fun—people driving underneath honked their horns. Some guy stopped on the side of the road and took a picture; I think he was from a newspaper or something. At the time, I didn't truly understand the importance of such a creative romantic gesture; I just thought my bro was funny and did funny silly things for his girlfriend.

As I grew up, I began to understand women, at least somewhat, and it was then I realized that my brother totally had it figured out. He knew how to create that excitement in his relationships. He knew how to keep the girls coming back for more.

Creative Date #51

Gazebo Dinner

Have you ever driven by a park and seen a Gazebo and thought that it would make a good place to have dinner? No? Well, call me weird, but that's what I think about when I drive by. They're usually in a really beautiful location, which makes a perfect setting for a candlelight dinner for two. This date idea is definitely not first date material; use this one to sweep your special someone off her feet, or set the hook deeper, to go back to the fishing analogy.

What the date entails is you making dinner or buying it and setting it aside, probably at your house. Pick up your date and blindfold her. Tell her you found a really nice restaurant that you want to take her to, and then drive around until you get to the park or wherever the Gazebo is located. Special note about this date – if you have done a few of these creative ideas already with your date, the whole blindfolding trick may not work, so you'll have to think of some other way to get to where you want to end up by making up an excuse, or just say that you want to go to a park to chat before dinner.

Make sure that beforehand a table has been set up with a tablecloth and candles, plates, etc. Have a friend dressed up as a waiter guarding the table. When you show up, they seat you and you take off the blindfold. If you want to get really creative, make menus and have them on the table, as well. Your friend serves you for the evening and you and your date enjoy the dinner together. After you've finished eating, you can leave, or play some music and dance. Personally, I like the dancing idea. Slow dancing with someone you really like or love is a great way to spend the evening. Combine this with the star gazing date and it will be a night to remember for sure.

What you need for this date:

You need several things. A Gazebo in a great location—usually they are placed in a park or a flower garden, or near a housing complex. Then you need a card table that you can easily set up and that will fit in the Gazebo. Sometimes they already have a table in them. Next you need a tablecloth and place setting for the meal. Candles and candleholders will make the dinner even more special. For the food, pick a favorite meal. Have flowers as the centerpiece on the table. Play nice classical music during dinner and then maybe her favorite love song mix while you dance. You also need something to blindfold her with—a handkerchief works nicely.

My commentary on this date:

I don't know why I think about having a romantic dinner at a Gazebo every time I drive by one. I think I saw it done in a movie once and thought it was really spectacular. Eating dinner is usually mundane; you do it every night in the same place. Talk about boring. However, when you plan a creative dinner date, it brings excitement and adventure into the relationship, keeps your loved one intrigued, and builds the anticipation for the next time you'll surprise with a truly creative dinner. Also, make sure you don't prepare or buy food that you eat all the time. Macaroni and cheese is just not going to cut it. Learning how to cook isn't as hard as you think; make sure to check out my cooking channel on YouTube, *In the Kitchen with Matt,* for some great ideas.

Creative Date #52

Dinner Around the World in One Night

I got the inspiration for this date from the movie *It's a Wonderful Life*. Jimmy Stewart's character had a dream to see the world. He and his new wife were going to do just that for their honeymoon, but then circumstances arose so they couldn't go. So his wife decorated their home with posters from far away places.

How can you have dinner around the world in one night? Well, it's actually quite simple, but it takes planning and listening to the person that you care about. That is one key to success, or so I've been told; a good listener is way ahead of the game when it comes to love.

So for this date, find out all the places that your date would like to visit, such as Europe, the Caribbean, Australia, etc. Then go out and get posters of locations from each of those places. Yes, this is definitely one of the more expensive dates. Wherever you want to have your dinner, put up the posters all around the room, so it has the feel of a world traveler. Then make or have dinner there, and don't forget the details. If they like warm places, turn up the heat. If they like a colder location, such as snowboarding and mountains, change the temperature in the room fit the mood, as well as the lighting.

What you need for this date:

You need a lot of posters and whatever food you want to have. Prepare a lunch or dinner that would fit one of the places. For example, if they really wanted to go to China, you would have posters of China, and you would prepare Chinese Food. Be creative with it, try and make the room seem like you are actually in one of those places, and you could even dress the part, too, if she wants to go to Hawaii, have Hawaiian posters and wear flowered shirts and leis. The possibilities are endless.

My commentary with this date:

This date is a cool and creative idea, something different, better, special, a night to remember. These are the kinds of memories we'll carry with us for a long time, and even never forget. I was invited to a girl's birthday party several months ago, which had a French theme. She loved Paris, so the house was decorated correspondingly and food was prepared to fit that location. This particular occasion was not a date, but there was a great group of guys and girls there, flirting with each other, having a good time, and tasting that great French cuisine. Good times for sure!

Creative Date #53

All Aboard!

Cars have long since been the most popular mode of transportation. But why not try something different and take your date on a train? You can find some scenic rides that will take you through beautiful landscapes. Growing up in California near the coast, there is one particular train that starts out in the majestic Redwood forest, and winds up at the Santa Cruz Beach boardwalk. A park near my parent's house has a neat train that takes you all around the park for a nominal fee—I love that ride!

This type of date can be done in a group or with just you and your date alone. There are even long-distance train rides that you could take your spouse or significant other on. This is a perfect time to enjoy nature, chat with your date, and escape for the day or longer.

What you need for this date:

You need to look up the train's schedule—location, departure, and arrival. Sometimes they have train rides that are purely tourist rides. These are probably the ones that would be the most fun, unless you wanted to do a cross-country trip.

My experience with this date:

When I was in college in Utah, I heard about a train called the Heber Creeper. The Heber Creeper is a slow train that moves slowly along the foot of the mountains. The ride is roughly two hours long and offers some breathtaking views. One year, I heard that for homecoming they would be riding the Heber Creeper and that there would be a dance on it. I thought it would be really fun to invite a girl named Jen to go with me. I had actually taken her out a week before and she seemed to be interested in me, and since I was interested in her, I thought it should make for a fun evening.

I picked her up at her apartment; she looked amazing, like a princess from a fairytale. She locked her arm around mine and I escorted her to my car. We then drove the forty minutes to the restaurant, where they had no more seating available for the night. Whoops. We found ourselves at this castle-like inn. The food portions left much to be desired, but it really was like something out of a movie . . . when people in a movie go to a really fancy restaurant that charges lots of money for barely any food. It's alright, the food did taste good, even if it was pricey.

After dinner, we had only minutes left before the train was supposed to leave, but we arrived there just in time. Then our next problem was people. I had no idea this was going to be such a popular event, but we couldn't find a seat until we got to the very back of the train. There were both inside and outside cars; the outside ones were extremely chilly so we only sat there long enough to look at the moonlight as it danced across the rugged mountains. Then we were done—it was cold and neither of us had a jacket.

Once back inside, we danced a little bit and drank lots of hot chocolate. As we were dancing I could tell that she was interested in me. She wanted to dance close and holds hands while walking around. We joked and flirted with each other. On the drive home, however, I realized that I wasn't really interested in her. I couldn't explain it; she was cute and had a great personality. After arriving at her apartment, it was time for the awkward part: I walked her to her door and gave her a hug goodbye, there was a pause, and she looked at me as if to say, "Aren't you going to kiss me?" I never did ask her out again, I just didn't feel the connection I was looking for and did not want to lead her on. I had an excellent time on the date, though.

Creative Date #54

Horse and Buggy Ride

Probably one of the most romantic rides ever is a horse and buggy ride through the country or around the city at night.

These are often really popular in large cities during the Christmas season. They aren't very cheap, but the expense is worth it. There is something magical about riding in a horse driven carriage or buggy. The clattering of the hooves on the pavement and the man in the top hat make it feel like a fairytale. If you like fairytales and money is no problem when it comes to your special someone, then you definitely should take them on a carriage ride. Can't you see it? You put your arm around her, look up at the stars, while every passersby stares at you in envy—a wonderful way to share an evening. Oh, and maybe get a few kisses along the way, too.

What you need for this date:

You do not need to plan ahead much for this date; all you need to do is show up to where the horse and buggy is. You could make inquiries to see where the nearest buggy ride is to your location. This would be really nice to do in December, so you can see all the Christmas lights and decorations. Cities like New York and San Francisco stick out in my mind for great places to do one. Temple Square in Salt Lake City is another great location for a buggy ride. Make sure to dress appropriately for the weather.

My commentary on this date:

This date is one that has been used many times in the movies. My friend just went on one and he couldn't talk enough about how awesome it was. Once again this date is out of the ordinary; normally you would drive around, find a place to park, then walk to shops, etc. What could be better than scouting out the shops from inside a buggy? It is also a great excuse for cuddling. If you are with your spouse or significant other then I suppose you will already be cuddling, but if you haven't gotten to that stage yet with your date, here is a great opportunity to take it to the next step.

Creative Date #55

Write a Song and Sing It to Her

A really romantic thing to do for a girl is to write a song and sing it to her. Writing songs is no easy task, but it is amazing how the words seem to flow when you have someone you really care about in mind. I have never met a girl that wouldn't love it if a guy they really liked wrote a song especially for them. Now this is not a first date kind of thing. Well, it could be, if you wanted her to think you are a psycho and never speak to you again. This date works well with someone you are already in a relationship with, and who you want to express your feelings in a different way than just words or flowers.

What you need for this date:

You need nothing more than a computer or pen and paper, and your imagination. Then all you have to do is plan an evening when you want to surprise her with your song. Somewhere remote and beautiful, like in the mountains or on the beach, would make the date more romantic.

My commentary on this date:

One summer I was playing softball and met this really cool girl. We got along well and started dating, and about four dates in I was hooked. I was whooped, to say the least. I wrote a clever song to the tune of "Grow Old with You" by Adam Sandler. I chose that tune because on one of our dates we were both singing that song. The song went something like this:

"Close To You" lyrics by *Matt Taylor*

Based on the tune "Grow Old with You" by *Adam Sandler*

"I saw you standing there with a softball mitt,

I walked up to you and chatted a bit.

It was so nice being close to you.

I called you up on the telephone,

And as we talked I didn't feel alone,

It would have been so nice to be close to you.

And then I picked you up and we drove to the beach.

Went rock climbing, til time to eat.

All I wanna do is be close to you.

I'll think of you, smile at you, and sing you a song,

When you are sad. Hold you, love you, give you

A massage when your muscles feel bad.

Oh, I could be the man who is close to you.

Now it's getting hard not to think of you,
I hope that we will be together soon.
It would be so nice to be close to you.

I wanna be close to you."

She loved it, but alas, we didn't end up dating for very much longer. My oldest brother plays the guitar and while dating his girlfriend at the time, he wrote a song for her. He took her to the beach, set out a blanket, then ate food and watched the sunset. Then just as the sun was about to hide its face behind the horizon, he got out his guitar and sang her his song he wrote. She loved it! And why wouldn't she? Songs are almost guaranteed a good response.

Creative Date #56

Sunset Walk on the Beach

Who doesn't like long walks on the beach? If you've got even a speck of romance in you, the beach really is a spectacular place to have a date.

It is nice to get away from the city sometimes and walk down the shore, wiggle your toes in the sand, and listen to the waves crashing. However, it is a little difficult to have a date at the beach if you don't happen to live near one. With that said, it might be worth the trip, especially if the person you're taking really likes going to the beach. You could also find a lake and walk along the shore. If you're worried that a lake isn't romantic enough, you can fix that pretty easily—take your stroll at sunset. Sunsets always add a romantic, peaceful element to everything.

If you're lucky enough to be able to visit the beach, sit, relax, and enjoy the cool coastal breeze. You could even set out a blanket and take a nap, look at the stars, or whatever else you can think of.

What you need for this date:

Transportation to the beach is all you need. This is basically a free date, unless you have to travel. Bring what you want; if you are just going for a walk, you don't need much.

My experience with this date:

I have done this a couple of times with different girls, including one I really liked. Her name was Jenny, and on the drive up we listened to music, sang along, and chatted each other up. We arrived at the Boardwalk in Santa Cruz, California. After parking the car in paid parking—I really hate paying to park at places—we walked around on the boardwalk browsing the different shops. Next, we walked down the beach, took a seat in the sand, and just talked. It was a little chilly so we cuddled a bit—a huge bonus. All in all, it was another fantastic day at the beach.

After the beach excursion, we drove home and I invited her in to watch a movie. We watched *The Princess Bride*. During the movie, we cuddled and she placed her hand in mine. I might be clueless sometimes when it comes to signs, but a girl holding your hand is a pretty good indication that she likes you. At the end of the movie when the song by Willie Deville called "Storybook Love" began playing, I asked Jenny to dance. We started dating after that. For the first time in a while I thought I'd found someone remarkable. It was not to be, however. We dated for two more weeks when she suddenly pulled the plug. Dropped the good 'ol "F" bomb on me: "I just want to be friends." Well . . . at least the beach was amazing, right?

Creative Date #57

Formal Dances

I must admit, one of my favorite parts in fairytale movies and romantic comedies is when the princess, heroine, or whoever it is gets all dress up to go to the ball. Can't you picture it? She walks in and it seems like time stands still. The prince or hero takes a glimpse of her, an expression of awe on his face, speechless as he watches her advance through the room, the envy of every woman there, until she finally, after what seems like ages, approaches him with a smile that lights up the room.

For an elegant evening, take your date to a formal dance. Your college, church, high school, work, city, etc. could put it on. There are places around that put on very large formal dinners and dances; just look it up on the internet and you should find plenty of places where you can go.

This date is good for a few reasons. One, because it allows you to dress up. It is always nice to dress to the nines when the situation permits. I have heard from many of my female friends that they love the opportunity to dress up really nice once in a while. Two, dancing allows you to be close to your date, girlfriend, or wife, and who doesn't want that? Don't dance? Fake it 'till you make it. And slow songs are easy;

it's pretty simple to just stand there with your date in your arms and sway back and forth.

What you need for this date:

For this date all you need is to find out where the event is being held, and if you need to make reservations or buy tickets in advance, make sure that you do that.

My experience with this date:

In high school I had a major crush on a girl that happened to go to the same church as me. She went to the same high school as well, so I saw her quite a bit. She liked me when I was younger, but at the time I wasn't sure if I was interested in her. When I finally figured out that I did like her, she didn't like me. Anyway, we were always friends.

I moved out of the area for a few years and thought I was over her. When I returned to the area, the first time I saw her nearly knocked me out of my shoes. Her brother was a very good friend of mine and while he was over at my house one day he suggested that I ask his sister out. I thought that was an excellent idea. There happened to be a formal dance at our church and that would be a perfect date. I called her up and invited her to go. She accepted and seemed very excited to go with me. I was too—both extremely excited and nervous at once, because this would be the first time that I'd ever taken her out on a date.

I put on the best clothes that I had and borrowed my brother's car, since his was nicer than mine. I drove to her house and stood at her doorstep, butterflies doing a number in my stomach. Finally, I rang the doorbell. The door opened and my jaw dropped as I gazed upon the beautiful creature standing before me. She looked more gorgeous than ever. She gave me a big smile and we drove to the dance.

I was feeling pretty good about myself. I was on a date with a girl who had plagued my dreams for so long. She seemed to be digging me, too. We walked to the dance floor and said hello to some friends that we knew. Then a friend of hers told her that she had a phone call. She said that she would be right back. She didn't come back. Three hours passed and she still didn't come back. In fact, she didn't show up again until the end of the night when the music stopped and the lights came on. She was crying. Her ex-fiancée had shown up and she had talked to him the entire time. She apologized and said that she was sorry the whole drive back home. I walked her to her door where she gave me a big hug and called me a "gentleman." Great, thanks.

I later realized I should've acted more mad at her than I did, but it's okay; at least that date cured me of my crush on her.

Creative Date #58

Dinner in a Tree house

The key to being creative is doing ordinary activities in unusual places. Dates like these are great for spicing up a relationship and are usually more fun as well. One that's awesome is to have dinner up in a tree house. You can make it a simple dinner or an elegant one with candles and the works. Music would add to the atmosphere and allow dinner to be followed by dancing. Tree houses are pretty cool because they usually have a nice view, and it gives the date a Swiss Family Robinson or Tarzan flavor to it.

What you need for this date:

Well, for one thing, in order to have dinner in a tree house you need to have a tree house, or at least access to one. Which means you may need to do some searching online. Maybe you can find one in your area that you can rent, if you don't already know someone that has one. They aren't the most common of things to own. You also need extension cords that can run up there, unless it already has its own electricity. This lets you have light for your date, and can power a movie after your dinner. Make sure to have the table and everything set up beforehand. Good preparation makes a date go more smoothly.

My commentary with this date:

Ever since I was about 3 or 4 we had a tree house in our huge eucalyptus tree. The tree house was about 12 feet long and 8 feet wide. It wasn't a huge house, but perfect for us kids. The floor was about 18 feet off the ground. I never was able to have a date up in there, because by the time I started dating, the house was old and rickety. There was no telling what would happen if you went up there, let alone two people eating dinner. But my brother's friend used our tree house for a creative date with his girlfriend back in the day, and she absolutely loved the date. They even ended up married. Coincidence? I think not.

Creative Date #59

Paddle Boat Ride

Some lakes with parks around them have paddleboats that you can rent and ride around on. Rental prices are usually reasonable, and the boats provide a nice relaxing ride on the lake. This is a perfect time to enjoy the weather and have meaningful conversation with your date. You could get a group and have paddleboat races, or just compete between the two of you. This would work fine for a first date. If you want, bring some sandwiches and eat them as you paddle around the lake. Not only will you get to spend some valuable time with someone special, you will also get a bit of a workout it in. A win-win situation, if you ask me.

What you need for this date:

You just need to drive to a place that has paddleboat rentals. Make sure that you research beforehand the times and prices.

My experience with this date:

I grew up next to a few parks with big man-made lakes that offered paddleboat rides. Being young, I wasn't in the dating mindset, more like the "fun" mindset, and so never took advantage of the boat rentals. But after seeing a movie with a couple riding on a paddleboat, I realized that it would make a really fun date. Once I moved to Arizona, I found out that Tempe Town Lake has paddleboat rides. I took a girl out on one and we rode around the lake in style. It was pretty awesome. She liked it, but alas, she only wanted to be friends.

Creative Date #60

Blazin' Bonfires

A really romantic date that costs next to nothing is building a fire next to a lake at night. You can roast marshmallows, have hot dogs, or some other type of campfire food. Another thing you can do that's fun is playing music from a speaker, and—you guessed it—ask her to dance. If you're musical, play the guitar for her. Girls can't resist a good guitar. This could also be a perfect place to read a poem for her that you wrote, tell scary stories, or just cuddle up and watch the fire burn.

What you need for this date:

Nowadays there are fire warnings in certain areas, so before you go somewhere and plan on making a bonfire, make sure it's allowed. Usually it's okay if you're really close to a lake, because it would be quite impossible to burn the lake down. But make sure you double-check so you don't wind up getting a citation; nothing is more embarrassing then getting busted while on a date. Well, I guess there are a few things that would be more embarrassing, but I won't get into those.

My commentary on this date:

I've been to many bonfire activities. You can never go wrong with them—it's so nice to be outside and enjoy nature while basking in the warmth of a fire.

Several years ago, one of my best friends had a small group date where they wound up at the lake. They decided to make a fire. However, they didn't realize that there was a fire ban going on, and sure enough, the park ranger showed up. He issued them all citations, and they wound up having to do community service. Okay so not the best example, but it is an example of needing to be fully prepared. Always check to make sure it is okay to have a fire in the first place. Everyone loved the date up to the citation, but hey, they wound up doing the community service together, so I guess they were dating as criminals. I kid, I kid.

Creative Date #61

Romantic Getaway Weekend

I think a very fun thing to do with your spouse or significant other is to take them on a romantic weekend to a resort like Lake Tahoe, a beach town, Sundance, Telluride, Florida Keys, or anywhere else with a great place to stay.

Once there, you can plan out some of the dates I've outlined in this book like a candlelight dinner, a bonfire, or something else. You can rent bikes and go on a ride through the picturesque mountains, or paddleboat on a lake. The possibilities are endless. If there is a river nearby you can go rafting, or some places offer Para-sailing. You also can just do nothing; relax and sun bathe.

What you need for this date:

You probably want to book the cottage, cabin, or hotel room well in advance depending on the season and the location. Get a map so you don't get lost while driving there, and make sure to pack the necessities.

My commentary on this date:

One summer when I was still in college, two of my best friends and I planned a trip to Lake Tahoe. We decided that we wanted to spend about a week there so we could do as many things as possible. None of us had a ton of cash to spend so we were going to stretch our budgets as much as we could. We invited some of our college friends to make it a reunion, of sorts.

There was a married couple, an engaged couple, two single guys and a girl who came on the trip. I guess there was another guy, if you count the big Black bear in the area, but we only saw him once and he didn't come to the pool with us or play video games. Psssh . . . bears, no fun at all.

It was awesome. We went mountain bike riding through the picturesque countryside, hung out at the lake for a bit, went swimming at the clubhouse pool (no lake swims for us—Lake Tahoe is beyond freezing), and went on walk to look at the amazing homes that overlooked Lake Tahoe. Back at the house we cooked and ate scrumptious food, such as the barbecue shish kabobs I've mentioned, and lounged around enjoying each other's company. My friends took pictures with their digital cameras so the vacation could be well documented. There were some that turned out spectacular; one in particular was of a couple of us standing with the lake and the sunset behind us; it turned out so good that it looked as if it wasn't real. I later made a video slideshow of the trip that I know everyone appreciated.

The entire thing was so much fun chilling without a care in the world. Getaways are great.

The week wasn't romantic for me, but it could have been if it was just one couple there. One of my friends took his fiancée on a bike ride, along with several walks alone together. I am sure it was romantic for them.

Creative Date #62

Visit a Day Spa (Treat Yourself!)

For the hardworking don't-get-out-much married couple, or anyone, really, going to a day spa is sure to please you. In fact, you'll probably never want to leave.

Day spas are great for muscle and mental relaxation; they are a pleasant escape from the normal routine. They can be found in most locales, so you should have no problem finding one. Good day spas aren't cheap, but they are worth it. So as you can probably tell by now, this date is more on the expensive side. The really nice spas will have restaurants, massages (of course), saunas, hot tubs, swimming pools, and skin treatments of all types. Basically, enough activities to where you could spend a whole day there.

What you need for this date:

Look up a few online to find some good ones in your area. Yelp is a handy site for seeing reviews and such. Also, you'll need to plan your budget accordingly, and if it's tight, might want to plan a DIY spa date, instead.

My commentary on this date:

Years ago when I was in college, one of my good buddies, Robert, called me up and wanted me to babysit his 2-week-old baby. Whoa, only two weeks old and they wanted me to babysit for them, they must be doing something really cool. Since I'm trustworthy and experienced in the ways of babysitting, I said that I would be happy to take care of the little tyke while they were out.

Robert took his wife Rebecca to a day spa to get massages. I haven't had kids or a pregnant wife, but I know how stressful it can be, and how many sleepless nights they probably had. So it is no wonder he wanted to take her somewhere special so they could relax and not worry about the baby. When they returned home about four hours later, they looked refreshed and ready to continue the raising of their child. Robert told me that I needed to do it sometime. I told him to hurry and hook me up with a girl so I could do that.

Creative Date #63

Flying and Dining: a "Movie Star" Date

The movie star date is quite the extravagant date, and likely the most expensive one in this book, but one that surely will be remembered and win you more brownie points than you can handle.

First, research some of the most exotic or romantic restaurants in the country, then call and make reservations for the one that you think will be the winner. Some restaurants of this nature will need to be reserved a couple weeks (or months) in advance. After you have done that, buy two round trip plane tickets to that destination. You can leave and come back on the same day, or spend the weekend there as well. Have a limo reserved and waiting when you arrive and see some of the sites before going to the restaurant. Make sure the limo picks you up afterwards and takes you back to the airport or to the nice hotel you've picked out. The idea is to have your date feel like she is a movie star for the day/weekend. Let her experience the life of luxury.

What you need for this date:

You need to find some cool restaurants, which can be done by browsing the web. You need to make reservations with the restaurant and limo service, and also with a hotel if you are staying that long. Have the limo driver bring flowers to give to your date. If you really wanted to be clever you could tell the waiter or waitress, without your date knowing, to ask one of the other patrons to walk up and ask her for her autograph. If you book a hotel room, have flowers, chocolates, and maybe a fondue fountain set up in the room for you when you return from the evening's activities.

My commentary on this date:

I have heard of people doing something similar to this where they fly somewhere and eat, walk around a bit, then fly home all in the same day. I have never had the money or someone special enough to do a date like this. I wanted to make sure, however, that readers of all income levels had creative date ideas, not just all expensive or cheap or even free dates. I love this idea and can't wait to plan something like this for my future significant other or spouse. This might be a great anniversary date as well, and is of course perfect for a proposal.

Creative Date #64

Rose Petal Delight and a Packaged Treat

For a very special evening, like a night to propose, or an anniversary or birthday, do this fun date involving rose petals for the one you love.

This is definitely one for couples that are in love, not for someone you just met. The idea goes like this: Get into your significant other's house (if you're not already married), and place rose petals all around the entryway where she will first walk in. Make a trail leading to the middle of the living room where scented candles are lit, and in the middle, a huge box waiting to be opened. Plan to be in the house or apartment, but hiding of course—maybe you can film it on your phone. This will work well if she has a set time when she gets home each day.

When she arrives she will most definitely follow the trail of petals and will open the big present. Inside will be a smaller present, then inside that a smaller present, and so on and so forth, until finally getting to the last box, which is your special gift. If this date sounds familiar then you probably have seen the movie *Serendipity*, which happens to be one of my favorite romantic comedies.

What you need for this date:

You need a lot of rose petals; you could probably call the flower shop ahead of time and ask them to save some for you, otherwise you will have to buy all the roses and pluck the petals yourself. Sometimes the shops already have packages of rose petals ready to go. Then you will have to buy scented candles, as well. It is up to you how many boxes you want to wrap, but I think the more there is the more anticipation there would be. All that is left to buy is the present. It could be an engagement ring, an anniversary necklace or ring, or maybe something silly for her birthday. If you are going through all the effort and expense I would make the gift pretty special. Your date will definitely be the envy of all her friends.

My commentary on this date:

I experience this date every time I watch the movie *Serendipity*. My movie world collides with my real life world and then I realize this type of thing doesn't only have to be done in the movies. The date isn't too complex to think up, it isn't some off the wall incredibly genius date either, it is merely a creative romantic date that anyone can do if they put enough time and effort and a little expense into it.

Chapter 4: Adventure and Miscellaneous Dates

"Not even the sky is the limit"

Sometimes when you get right down to it you don't necessarily want to plan a romantic date specifically, although any date in any location could be romantic. This next chapter deals with dates that I would consider adventurous, with some other miscellaneous ideas thrown in. These dates will most likely appeal to the thrill seekers, the adventure junkies, or even the homebodies that want to just get out and do something.

Creative Date #65

Kiddie Pool Rafting

When I first heard of this idea I thought the people were crazy. Who would think up something like river rafting in a blown-up kiddie pool? Yes, that's right, this group date activity involves rafting down a river in a kiddie pool.

It's up to you how strong a current you go down, but it is not recommended to go down any river that has Class 1 or bigger rapids. It is more of a floating experience. To make it more creative, use brooms for paddles. What??? Brooms for paddles, are you serious? You heard me right; brooms work fine as paddles and make the whole experience much more unique.

What you need for this date:

You need a kiddie pool—the kind that holds air in the sides. You can get them at Wal-Mart or a similar store, along with the hand-pump and brooms. Next, you need your bathing suits and a river to raft down. You will probably want to bring sunscreen, and possibly sandals or river shoes.

Next, take two cars to the river, one to leave where you will get off the river after rafting and the other to take you up the river where you will cast off. Finally, you will need your adventuring spirit, because it is quite a ride. The trick is to sit on the sides and not on the bottom of the pool. The bottom is too thin and if the river is at all shallow, you will bump your butts on the rocks, which doesn't feel too great. Sit on the sides and allow your feet to gently flow over any obstacles that happen to come under the pool as you float.

Note: No more than 6 passengers will work in the kiddie pool raft.

My experience with this date:

It was summer time; the hot desert air blew gently against my face. It was a Saturday, and my roommate's girlfriend had come into town. He wanted to show her a good time so he asked me if I had any ideas. Thinking back on a fond experience, I told him about kiddie pool rafting. He was ecstatic. Of course he was. I am a creative mastermind.

We bought the necessary items and invited our other roommate, Joey, to come along. He wanted to bring a date and we said it was fine. We packed the gear, picked up the girls, and set out on a summer adventure. I decided to play river guide for my two friends and their dates—yeah, I was the fifth wheel— but in this case I didn't mind. The river we decided to float down was the ominous, class 0, fly fisherman infested, Provo River. I had gone down it before, so it was a good choice. The first time I went down we plowed into a stick that popped our pool, so we didn't get to go down the whole way, but this time being the experienced kiddie pool rafter that I was, it was a different story.

We piled into the raft and pushed off the shore. I took the time to instruct them how to paddle with a broom and how to sit on the raft. The water was chilly, the air was hot, and the fish were jumping. As we made our way down the canyon river, I couldn't help but notice the majestic mountains around us—it was superb.

Then the rapids came. Nothing to brag about, but for a kiddie-pool it might be trouble. We narrowly escaped capsizing; however we did get a small hole in the bottom of the raft. Since it was the part that was just thin plastic and didn't hold any air, I wasn't worried. We quickly noticed that although we were fortunate with our maneuvering, a girl in front of us wasn't so lucky. She had managed to wrap her one-person plastic boat around a fairly large tree branch that hung over the water. She was hanging on for dear life—okay, maybe that's a bit of an exaggeration, but makes for a better story. Her raft was useless, and since she was soaked and the water was frigid we decided to pull over and give her a ride, as long as she made good use of the broom and pulled her weight.

We laughed and talked the rest of the way. After the 3 hour-long float we made it to the end and out. The girl we rescued asked her brother who had been waiting for us to take me up to my car, which was a nice gesture and saved me having to walk all the way back, since we didn't bring two cars. I never saw the girl again, but I am sure she won't forget the time she was saved by a bunch of college students. This experience is probably one of my favorite college experiences. Where I live now in Arizona, the Salt River is a very popular floating destination, and one that would work great for something like this.

Creative Date #66

Caving and Exploring

Ever have the desire to be like Indiana Jones or one of the Goonies? Crawling around in caves looking for neat stuff is not everyone's cup of tea, but I know there are a lot of people who enjoy that kind of an adventure. The fear of being in an enclosed area with darkness, the fear of the unknown, the really cool rock formations underground, the sure joy of being in the earth, are all reasons one might or might not want to go spelunking or "caving."

Bringing a group to a cave for a date can be a very exciting thing. You could plan some kind of scary event that will take place and really freak out your dates, or just explore the area. An outing like this will not work really well if your date is claustrophobic or hates to get a little dirty. You could take candles in with you and tell scary stories. There really is a lot of stuff that you can do in a cave. Keep an eye out for critters though, I have found Gila monsters, bats, and rattlesnakes in the caves here in Arizona.

What you need for this date:

Gas money, a car, and a place to go are all you need. If you want to bring food in with you make sure to pack that as well, and bring plenty of flashlights and candles if you want them. This is a really cheap and fun exciting thing to do. Some places you might want to search for caves are here: http://cavern.com/, http://www.showcaves.com/english/usa/caves/ or you can just do a basic Google search to find a cave near you.

My commentary on this date:

On one occasion, I took a girl hiking with the end goal in mind to go to the "bat cave." No, it was not Batman's lair. It was an old abandoned mine in the Superstition Mountains of Arizona. Since moving to Arizona, this hike had been one of my favorite places to explore. I have taken a few dates to that spot over the years until the mine was finally boarded up. On this particular date when we got to the mine, I had the idea that it would be fun to light candles and place them as we walked, then when we got to the end, we would walk back with only the candle light to guide us, instead of using our flashlights. It was awesome!

I have been an avid cave explorer ever since I was a wee lad. My buddies and I would climb around in drains, sewers, and pretty much anywhere we weren't supposed to I quickly learned that real caves are the best. Some of my favorites are Moaning Caverns in California, Pinnacles National Park in California, Peppersauce Cave in Arizona, and Nutty Putty Caves in Utah. I have yet to explore the really big caverns such as Carlsbad Caverns, which are located in New Mexico, or Mammoth Cave, which is in Kentucky.

I went with a group to the Nutty Putty Caves and that was a blast. When I was young, about 16, our Boy Scout troop went to Moaning Caverns. I was excited because I heard that it offered a 180-foot rappel down the cave with a guided spelunking tour afterward. I waited in anticipation until it was my turn, then I noticed a very cute 17-year-old girl that showed up with her family. She was the only one that wanted to go on the tour through the earth, so she joined our group. That made me even happier. It was my turn; I locked the karabiner to my harness and used the nifty rappelling device and descended into the world below.

It was incredible down inside the earth. There were stalactites and stalagmites and the cave actually moaned. The group gathered, the girl included, and we set out crawling after our guide. The girl ended up hanging out with me the whole time; of course she would, as I was an experience spelunker and a good-looking one at that. One of the leaders was a little too plump and couldn't quite get through a particular part, so he had to turn back. The girl and I kept our pace and explored some of the not-so-popular areas. Once we emerged from the dark tunnels, we climbed the long spiral staircase, which led to fresh air and the normal world. I would have liked to have gotten her number, but much to my chagrin, I failed to do so.

Creative Date #67

Sweet Sounds of the Symphony

For a more elegant date you could go to a nice restaurant for dinner, then afterwards go to the symphony.

Needless to say, this night is one for the classy. It lets your date know that you enjoy the finer things in life, like good music, and it also shows that you are somewhat cultured and are willing to do something other than the ordinary dinner and a movie date. In my experience most girls enjoy the symphony, but of course if your date, girlfriend, or spouse doesn't like that sort of thing this is probably not the best date idea. There are also some really cool "themed" symphonies you can go to. The music of "Harry Potter" is one that comes to mind here in Arizona. Another themed event in Phoenix is "Star Wars vs. Star Trek: The Music of Deep Space." If your date happens to be a Science Fiction fan, or loves Harry Potter, either one of those ideas could work.

What you need for this date:

It is always good to purchase tickets for events like this in advance for two reasons. You don't run the risk of having it sell out, and you won't have to wait in line to get the tickets. Some symphonies may not allow the pre-purchasing of tickets; if that is the case you will probably want to get there early. It might be a good thing to do for an anniversary or some other special day, or if you don't mind spending the money you can do it anytime that there are performances. Of course there are always ways to make the date a little cheaper. If you make dinner at home or pick a cheaper restaurant it will cost less, but sometimes you just want to spend money on a really nice evening.

My experience with this date:

I chose to do this as a group date one winter evening in Utah. One of my friends wanted to set me up with a friend of hers who actually grew up in the same town that I did. I was very curious to see who this girl was, and I was excited to experience the Utah Symphony. The time came for me to meet my date. When I saw her, I recognized her as someone whom I met a while ago in California. We both laughed and then met the other people in the group who were going to join us.

We picked a moderately priced Mexican restaurant near the symphony hall. We had a really nice dinner. My date, Lisa, was looking cute, smiling at me, and making pleasant conversation throughout dinner. Afterwards we made our way down the few blocks to the symphony. It was incredible; I always enjoy classical music but had never before heard it live. It was amazing.

We had a really good time. There was good flirting going on during the symphony. I jokingly put my arm around her and could have left it there if I wanted. I held back, though. I was attracted to her, but for some reason it didn't click for me. I can't really explain it, only that sometimes I get a gut feeling that tells me not to date a person anymore.

I haven't always followed my gut, which leads to even more troubles, so I have learned to follow it.

Creative Date #68

It's Play Time

Not all of the date ideas that I share with you will be incredibly creative. However, they will be something that you probably don't do all the time. For example, this next idea is a good change of pace from seeing a movie. It's similar to the symphony date, but instead, you could go to a play. Plays are normally more expensive than movies but some people enjoy them much more.

What you need for this date:

Similar to going to a symphony, if you need to get tickets in advance then do it, otherwise you might get stuck with terrible seats or not being able to get in at all. Normally you can check the local entertainment section in your newspaper to find when and where plays are being performed. If you are in college you can check the information desk in your fine arts building to find out when their plays are being held, or they will probably have a website set up for special events and such.

My experience with this date:

I have actually gone on several dates to plays and on all those occasions I didn't once regret going; it was really fun each time. One time I took a girl on Halloween to an outdoor castle theater, and we watched the play *Sweeney Todd*—it was incredible. *Sweeney Todd* is about a man who runs a barbershop but winds up killing his patrons and then baking them in pies. This happened to be our second date; I knew the girl liked me and I liked her as well. We had blankets and cuddled together during the play. After a very enjoyable evening, I kissed her goodnight and we started dating. But . . . then I got that unlucky feeling again in the pit of my stomach screaming to be free, which meant one thing: no more dating her. A gut is a funny thing, I tell you. One minute it's buzzing with butterflies, the next there's a pit there. Love is crazy.

Creative Date #69

Go to an Opera or Musical

An opera is one of those really cultured events you only ever see people in movies going to. They seem to be more expensive than symphonies and plays, but usually come with much more entertainment, extravagant costumes, and grandeur. The atmosphere and spectacle are different than a play and symphony, and can lend itself to quite the experience. A really popular one to go to is *La traviata*. If Opera's aren't your thing go to a musical instead, *Wicked*, or *Phantom of the Opera* would be great choices.

What you need for this date:

Just like the play or symphony, you probably want to get the tickets in advance. The tickets are all you need for this date.

My experience with this date:

My roommate's girlfriend set me up with her friend many years ago while I was in college. I had actually met the girl before at a party, so it wasn't going to be a blind date. I was already attracted to her and wanted to go out with her. I knew she liked the opera, so when I found out that one was playing at my college, I told her about it. She was excited and couldn't wait for the experience.

I picked her up and took her to the opera house. She wasn't flirty at all, but the conversation was flowing naturally so I thought that I still had a chance with her. The opera was fantastic. It was the first time I had ever gone to one. Later, we went to a restaurant for dinner; an all you can eat Brazilian place. All you can eat meat places are one of my favorite places to go. Can you picture me as a caveman? That's what I feel like when I'm there. My date had said she liked meat and had never been to that restaurant, so I knew I had to turn her into a caveman like me. Well, cave*woman,* I guess.

Creative Date #70

Festivals and Conventions—They're So Hot Right Now

There are many different festivals going on during the year, which make a great opportunity for a date.

My favorites are the Renaissance Fairs/Festivals and ComiCons. The type of festivals available will depend on your locale. In California where I grew up, there was a Renaissance Faire, Strawberry Festival, Garlic Festival, and of course the International ComiCon down in San Diego. They are quite entertaining. You probably want to go on a Saturday because it can be an all day event. If you go to the Renaissance Faire, make it more exciting and dress up. There you can see jousting, jugglers, eat all kinds of food, watch sword fights, almost as if you lived in the Middle-Ages. It is well worth the price of admission, especially if you really like that type of festival.

Some are free, like the Strawberry festival, where you just walk around, with the option of paying money for certain food or activities. There are usually live bands playing, as well. ComiCons are a whole different story. They usually last over a few days, and are full of exhibits, panels, food, costumes, and contests. Oh, and don't forget the freaks. Elaborate and crazy costumes reign at this place, some to the point of being legitimately freaky.

Of course there will be movie and TV stars there as well; maybe your date happens to like one of the celebrities that will be signing autographs. Imagine the points if you take them to meet their favorite star!

What you need for this date:

You may need to buy your tickets beforehand, but other than that you do not need much. Events like the Cons usually have special pricing for tickets that are bought ahead of time, and you will definitely want to plan ahead if you plan on going to the convention the whole time and are going to book a hotel as nearby hotels tend to sell out early.

My commentary on this date:

I had the opportunity to go to my first festival ever, which happened to be the Renaissance Faire in California. I had recently made a medieval costume for a short film that my brother and I made, so I decided to wear that to the festival. I was really excited. My parents drove, and my sister, my brother, his wife, and his friend all came with us.

When we arrived, the first thing I noticed is that other people were dressed up besides me. I felt proud to belong to such an elite group of costumers. I also noticed several couples holding hands, laughing, and enjoying each other's company. I was only 15 at the time so I was not really too concerned with girls yet. We walked around and looked at all the neat shops and little plays going on. There were sword fights, minstrels walking around, and people trying to act with an English accent. My favorite was the jousting arena, which consisted of bleachers that made an oval around a dirt field, something like the beginning of the movie *A Knight's Tale*, only the song "We Will Rock You" wasn't playing. Which is a shame, really—it would've made it perfect.

Here in Arizona I usually try and go each year to the Renaissance Festival in my area. It is always a good time, but I haven't taken a date there yet. Someday. One of my new traditions is to attend the Phoenix ComiCon each year in the summer. I love it. I haven't dressed up yet for one, but will most likely do that one of these years.

Creative Date #71

Hot Air Balloon Ride

For a really fun and exciting creative adventure, take your date on a hot air balloon ride. Not the cheapest of dates or adventures, but it's amazing and well worth the money.

Can you imagine soaring 500 to 1000 feet above the ground, watching the breathtaking view around you? This is the type of thing you'll talk about for a long time. Since it's pricey, it could be the type of date that you save up for and plan for a special day like an anniversary, honeymoon, birthday, or Valentine's day How about proposing to your special someone high above the land? That's a guaranteed yes, right there.

What you need for this date:

You will have to find out which hot air balloon company you'll want to use, which can easily be found online. If you have to drive very far it could easily become a whole day event, so plan accordingly.

My commentary on this date:

A buddy of mine took his girlfriend on a hot air balloon ride once. They totally dug the experience, they said it was probably one of the most thrilling adventures they'd ever had. They couldn't get over how amazing it was to fly above scenic mountains, forests, and lakes. Incredible, simply incredible.

Creative Date #72

Indoor Climbing Gym

Something really fun and active to do on a date is going to an indoor climbing gym. It is an excellent first date idea, but certainly can be done at any point in a relationship.

What's cool about the indoor rock climbing gym is that you get a controlled atmosphere, which is nice when you live somewhere with extreme temperatures. There's experienced workers there who can help you, plus you get a sense of accomplishment after making it to the top of the wall. Rock climbing gyms have become increasingly popular around the world. There are even rock walls on cruise ships, as well as portable climbing walls that are brought to special events. The cost for an indoor gym is moderately priced; it usually falls between $10 and $20 per person for a day pass, and can spend as much time there as you want. You can climb in the morning, leave, then come back later and climb some more. Make a day of it!

What you need for this date:

Bring your own climbing shoes, chalk bag, and harness, if you have them, otherwise you will have to rent gear there. Most big cities have a rock climbing gym; I know of at least 3 that are in a reasonable distance from where I live now in the greater Phoenix area.

My experience with this date:

I have taken many girls to the climbing gym on dates. For me it is a fun first date activity because you get to do something exciting while also having casual time to chat and get to know one another better.

One evening I was at a restaurant with my buddies, and I thought that one of the hostesses was cute. I, being the wimp that I was at the time, decided not to do anything about it. However, my friends weren't letting me off that easy, so they went back in and got her number and gave it to me. Hey, the less work you have to do to get a number the better, right? Yeah, I know. Lazy. Anyways, I called her up a few days later and asked her out. I told her that we were going to go to the climbing gym.

We did a double date. She was in excellent shape and climbed quite well for her first time, and of course was the cutest girl there that day. Even though we obviously didn't end up together, I thought that the date went well—we even went out a few more times after that. So basically, the climbing gym jump-started our fun, although short, dating life.

Creative Date #73

Horseback Riding

Ever get the urge to be a cowboy for a day? Take a date and go horseback riding. See what it would be like if you lived in the olden days before the invention of the automobile, when horses were the main mode of transportation.

Horseback riding is a good outdoor activity to do with a date. It is a chance to get away from city life and enjoy the surrounding landscape. It's also a pretty interesting experience, and one that most people want to do again. Make sure to bring apples for the horses, and don't forget treats for your date. Never forget those treats.

What you need for this date:

Just find stables that offer horseback riding for the public. This date can be a bit more expensive than other types, but is worth the money.

My commentary on this date:

When I was younger, I went camping with my friend and his parents. We stopped up in the Sierra Nevada Mountains at a place called Lake Alpine, which happens to be one of the most beautiful lakes I have ever been to, and we entered a fishing derby. The fishing was great that day, my friends, just great. We caught our share of trout, but this one fish, I tell you, must have been the size of a tuna. It tugged at my line, and I tugged back. This fish wasn't going to get the better of me. Moby Dick was nothing compared to this creature. The line strained under the weight, but still it held. After what seemed like hours, actually 5 minutes, I brought the gigantic trout to the surface and pulled it next to the rocks. My buddy grabbed the gigantic fish, but it squirmed loose and the hook broke, freeing my exceptional foe.

I would have won the tournament that day, but instead, I took third place and my buddy took fourth place. And guess what our prize was? Horseback riding! We showed up at the designated meeting place the next day. Being the keen observer that am, I noticed that many of the people there were couples. I knew I had to store away the idea for future dates.

The ride, my first, was stunning as we wound our way through the majestic Sierra Nevada Mountain range at an elevation above 8,000 feet. It was three hours of adventuring. I still remember my horse's name: Mary. Good times. Pretty much every state in the nation has great riding options available. I know that several of my friends have gone on this kind of date and can't wait to do it again.

Creative Date #74

Plane or Glider Ride

Some smaller airports offer plane or glider rides. This would be a really fun activity for a date.

Be aware that is pretty expensive, around the same cost as going on a hot air balloon ride. These rides allow you to fly in a craft much smaller than you have probably experienced. Make it even more exciting by having the pilot do some aerial acrobatics with you in the plane. If you and your date are squeamish when it comes to heights or being cooped up in a small area high above the ground, I don't think you would like this. But if the thrill of soaring up in the clouds like a bird fancies you, then this is right up your alley!

What you need for this date:

It's pretty easy to find a plane ride just through a simple internet search. All you need to do is show up, sit back, relax, and enjoy the ride.

My commentary on this date:

During college I had an opportunity every Thanksgiving to participate in a date auction. The group raised money for Sub-For-Santa, which is an organization that helps provide memorable Christmases to the less fortunate. The auction was set up where dates were auctioned off and the winner would give the money to Sub-For-Santa. There was always a Thanksgiving feast involved as well, which I looked forward to every year.

An acquaintance of mine, who was a pilot, offered a one-hour plane ride to a lucky girl one year. The excitement escalated as the price for the date went up and up and up. The girl who won paid over $100 for the date. Later, I found out from her that soaring through the clouds and over the mountains was an experience like no other. She totally loved it. Now if only I was a pilot and owned a plane . . .

Creative Date Idea #75

Neighborhood Safari

Not everyone has the time or the money to go on a safari through Africa. If you do have the money, then it would be pretty rad, no? Exhilarating, magical, insanely cool, would be the words I'd use to describe an actual safari.

For us mere mortals who can't fly to Africa for a date, a very nice alternative is getting in the car and driving to the nearest zoo, where you have all the exotic animals that you can look at without the hassle of a time-consuming trip. The zoo has always been a fun place to go for all ages. Why is it so appealing? Well, there are all sorts of cool animals to look at, there are usually interesting shows to watch, and there is plenty of time to chat with your date. Zoo prices are usually pretty reasonable, as well.

What you need for this date:

The only thing you need to do is make sure that the zoo is open the day you want to go.

My commentary on this date:

I have gone to the zoo on several occasions with family and in groups. When I was a teenager, I went with a group of friends to an Aquatic Zoo called Marine World, which is located in California. I was with one of my best friends and his cousins, one of which I had a crush on. Her name was Jill.

Jill and I got along pretty well at the zoo. There wasn't any real flirting going on, but the conversation was good. At least, she seemed to be interested in what I had to say. It was a great atmosphere for us to get to know each other and for me to decide if I wanted to ask her out. The animals were interesting, especially the tigers that we saw. Fun fact about Matt: Tigers have always been my favorite of the big cats. Now back to dating.

I never really asked Jill out, because I was young and stupid and afraid of females. I found out later that she was kind of interested in me. However, I happened to be out of the country for a long period time, and even though we corresponded through "snail mail," she lost interest and stopped writing me.

Creative Date #76

The Magical World of Theme Parks

Theme parks are awesome for dates. They offer all sorts of activities: roller coasters, arcades, fun games, shows, etc. Most people have been to some kind of theme park, whether it was Disneyland or Six Flags. It's definitely an activity that can be enjoyed by all ages. It is pure fun. And the food! Who doesn't like funnel cakes, corn dogs, popcorn, and cotton candy?

What you need for this date:

A whole lot of money, as crappy as that sounds. The price of admission has gone through the roof, it seems. Especially for places like Disneyland and Universal Studios; you can easily spend over 140 bucks for one ticket. But the experience is totally worth it.

My experience with this date:

I have taken three or four girls to theme parks for dates. Never the same theme park, so at least I got a variety. Probably the coolest one that I went to was at Medieval Times in Los Angeles. My girlfriend at the time wanted to do something fun and out of the ordinary. Since I had always wanted to go to Medieval Times in LA, I decided to take her there.

We arrived and noticed that the workers were dressed up like they lived a thousand years ago. The whole atmosphere was incredible; a real delight for my date and me. Soon we were seated around a big arena. There was an opening ceremony with the knights and a short play was performed for us while the servers brought us food, which consisted of big legs of turkey, ham, and potatoes. As we ate, we enjoyed jousting and other medieval games. As far as the girl goes, I continued to date her for a little while longer, but in the end we broke up. It just wasn't meant to be.

Creative Date #77

Get Your Laugh On!

Another of my favorite date ideas is going to a comedy club. Comedy clubs are excellent for first dates, as well as group dates, or even if you have been married for twenty years. The tickets are usually very reasonable, often between $8 and $10 per person.

As far as content goes, the ones I have gone to were family friendly. I am sure there are a variety of clubs out there that would suit your particular taste, just do a little research.

What you need for this date:

You need to find out where the clubs are, which should be easy with a simple internet search. It is always a good idea to call and make reservations. Some nights they sell out, and it wouldn't be a very fun date if you waited in line for only to find out that they were full.

My experience with this date:

I have taken girls to comedy clubs on many occasions. For most of them it was a first time experience. And it seemed to be a hit, as all of them told me afterward that they had a ton of fun. Of course it was fun, who doesn't like a good laugh once in a while?

Recently I took a girl named Emily to a comedy club called Jesterz. This place is a unique type of comedy experience. Instead of just sitting and laughing at the jokes of a comedian on stage, the audience gives suggestions to the comedians, who in turn make up some sort of funny scene right there on the spot. The audience participation is what makes this place awesome. So Emily and I went and enjoyed an awesome show. Afterwards, we went to a park and walked around the lake and talked. A perfect first date.

Creative Date #78

Treasure Caching – Geo Caching

Ever want to be like Indiana Jones and search for real treasure? Well now you can, and you can do it as a date or a group activity.

This idea is called treasure caching, also known as geo caching. What is a treasure or geo cache? Well, it's a place somewhere on the earth where someone has buried or hidden small treasures. Not usually something of great value, but the thrill of it is not really what you find—it's the steps that it takes to find it. If you are really into it you can go to a website called www.geocaching.com, where you'll find a list of many geo caches that you can search for. There is a catch, however: you need a GPS system to look for these caches, or the Geocaching app for your phone. For a group date idea, divide the group into two teams. Have each team come up with a treasure hunt; include riddles, clues, etc., to help the other team find it. If you want to get creative, make them use a compass as well. Then have something cool for them to find. If you do the Geo Caching at the above website, make sure that you have something to replace the treasure with; that way anyone else who looks for it will have something to find as well. Then end the evening with a treasure-hunting movie like *National Treasure*, the ultimate treasure hunting experience.

What you need for this date:

This date takes a lot of planning if you want to create your own treasure hunt. Otherwise, you need a GPS system or the app if you want to look for the already-hidden caches. Travel will also take planning, depending on what you decide to do. The app will be more limited, but if you make a treasure hunt yourself then the possibilities are endless.

My experience with this date:

I searched for my first geo cache while in college. It was a multi-cache meaning there is more than one place where you need to look for clues and items. It was really fun. I felt like a treasure hunter; it even had a bit of a *Da Vinci Code* feel to it. My friends that were with me were really into it as well. We had an incredible time as we tried to solve the riddles and find the clues, which would lead us to the next clue, and ultimately the treasure. My friends couldn't stop talking about it with everyone they saw—it really was a hit.

Years later in Arizona my friend and his date planned a treasure hunting activity for us, complete with all the clues. We didn't need a GPS system or anything like that, which made it easier and more fun. It was an awesome, creative way to spend the evening with a date and some friends.

Creative Date #79

Hook, Line, and Sinker

You know you've found a quality girl if she likes to go fishing. Even if she's never gone but is still willing to go, it's pretty dang cool.

It is quite a thrill to catch a fish, especially a big one. For a group or just the two of you, go fishing to a nearby river or lake. Bring a picnic basket and lunch with you, relax, throw out the line, and wait for a fish. You can bring books to read, cards to play, or a radio to listen to while you are waiting for a bite. However, if you are like me, you prefer fly-fishing or fishing with lures, which is a constantly-moving type of fishing with little breaks. This type lets you go to some pretty breathtaking areas while you cast your line over and over again.

What you need for this date:

You will need a fishing license if you fish at a lake, stream, or on the shore of the ocean. You won't need one if you fish off a pier into the ocean, though. You'll need fishing poles and bait or lures, and anything else you would like to use. Bring a blanket or folding chairs to sit on if you are fishing from the shore.

My commentary on this date:

It all started back when I was a wee little lad about the age of 4 or 5. My dad took me fishing for the first time. I was "hooked" ever since. I have many fond memories going to Sea Cliff Beach in the Monterey Bay and fishing off a great big cement ship that had a pier attached to it, which sadly got destroyed by a massive storm a few years ago. I caught many a fish through the years on that pier. We also took many fishing trips to places in the Sierra Nevada's, Colorado Rockies, the deserts of Arizona, the cool southern California coast, and many other places both local and not so local.

My dad used to take my mom fishing. She didn't really fish, but she would sit by him and read a book while he fished. Isn't that cute? Anyways, it would be a fun thing to do with your spouse, significant other, or even just as a fun date. You know you got a winner when your date isn't afraid to touch the bait or clean the fish that you catch. And who knows, if you're lucky you might even catch her heart—just don't let the line break.

Creative Date #80

Feelin' a Little Sporty

Everyone loves sports, right? Alright, maybe I'm just reaching. Even if not everybody is a fan, there's usually some kind of sporting event that will suit the masses.

Many sports are available in most cities, like major league baseball games, hockey games, and of course, football. If you don't have pro sports where you are, there's always college games. These options are all great examples of different events you could go to on a date, whether it's just two of you or in a group. Do some research beforehand and find out what your date's favorite sport to watch is. She'll appreciate it, believe me.

Ticket pricing can be really expensive depending on where you sit—the closer you are, the more expensive it is. Nosebleeds aren't always bad, though; it's all about who you're with. Sometimes games can be free if it's a special event or you both go to the same college. An idea to make the date a bit of an adventure is to take some fun transportation there. You could go by light rail, train, subway, or something similar. I know from experience that riding the light rail is fun, especially if you don't do it often, and there's a huge bonus: you don't have to worry about parking!

What you need for this date:

You need your tickets. If it is a major event, they might sell out, so it is a good idea to get the tickets early.

My experience with this date:

Many years ago I was invited by a girl that I had been dating to see an Oakland A's game. Not my choice, as I am a Giants fan, but it was her favorite team. Ahh . . . the things I do for love. It was Mother's Day the next day and she was a mom of two children. I gave her flowers and a Tigger stuffed animal (did my research and found out she loves Tigger) before we drove to the game. Yeah, I got mad gift giving skills.

We got to the game and had a great time. The ballpark food was on point, the A's lost, my date wasn't happy, but I was grinning on the inside. A great way to spend the day. On other occasions I have taken girls to volleyball games and basketball games and they were all really fun. Some years ago here in Arizona, a girl that I had gone out with three times invited me to go to an ASU Football game. We had a lot of fun, and she was really interested in me, but again, love is a fickle thing and I wasn't feeling it for some reason.

Creative Date #81

Back to the Classics: Bowling

I had to include some of the age-old classic dates, so here is one of them: bowling. Most people enjoy a good game of bowling, so it is definitely a safe and fun date.

I'm sure you're all wondering how in the world this is creative, seeing that anyone can think of something like bowling. But hear me out. The creativity comes with dressing up. Have your date dress up with you like a cliché bowler, or you can wear outfits from the 70s or 80s. Basically, you can dress up however you feel like; you could go bowling in your Halloween costume if you wanted. Make things interesting and put a little wager on the game. The loser gives the other a back massage, or if you really like her, have the loser make the other dinner. This is a great way to guarantee another date even if you lose. Bowling is not that expensive, either, and can be a great group date activity.

What you need for this date:

You need a bowling alley. Simple, eh?

My experience with this date:

I have taken girls to the bowling alley on numerous occasions. I have gone with just the two of us, and as a group date as well. I have always had fun doing that. One time I met this girl at the climbing gym where I had a membership. It was her first time climbing. I later got her number and set a date up with her. She mentioned that she liked bowling, so I took her bowling. That's right, I listen.

We went to the college campus bowling alley, because it was cheap and pretty close to her apartment, and just a really nice place to bowl. She had told me that she was a pretty good bowler, so I was expecting some good competition. We started to play and, get this, I proceeded to bowl the best game of my life. I bowled 206 against the girl. I think she got 95. She was a cute girl, and I kind of liked her, but she never called me back after that. Maybe you shouldn't down right murder the other person's score when you take her bowling. Oops, my bad.

Creative Date #82

Good Ole Mini-golf

One of the most classic dates known to man is mini-golf, or as some places call it, putt-putt. This is a date that is done quite frequently and is really popular with the younger crowd, because it is cheap and usually pretty fun.

Again, you're probably thinking, *Duh, Matt, I could have thought of that.* Well here's where it gets more interesting. To make it more creative, put some kind of twist on the game, like make a rule that both of you have to be touching the putter when you putt, or that the person who loses each hole has to do some kind of dare. Wouldn't that be interesting? You just have to open your minds and think creatively, but I guess that is what this book is for, so now all you have to do is read it.

What you need for this date:

You will need a place to play. Games are pretty cheap, usually around $5 to $10 per person.

My experience with this date:

I have taken girls mini-golfing on occasion. I did it because it is a really safe fun first date, with a low-pressure atmosphere, and the cost is minimal. The key is that I had fun each time. Sometimes doing something simple like going mini-golfing is all that you need to have a great evening.

Creative Date #83

Get Out On that Ice

Ice-skating is a fun activity for a date, whether in a group or just the two of you. It is especially nice if it is really hot outside and you want to be somewhere cool. Great for Arizona folk like me.

This date is not necessarily creative, but then again you can make it as creative as you like. There's always dressing up, of course. Those Halloween costumes in your garage? Bring them out! And don't worry too much about price—skating rinks don't usually cost an arm and a leg.

Holding hands while skating is one of the benefits of being on the cold ice. Gotta keep your date's hand nice and warm. Just make sure you don't fall on top of each other . . . or maybe you'd like it. It could be the perfect time to laugh and stare into each other's eyes, and then you fill in the rest. Go get 'em, tiger.

What you need for this date:

All you need for this date is a place to go, and if you have your own skates, bring them.

My experience with this date:

When I was really young and could count the number of dates that I had been on on one hand, I asked a girl named Kelly to go ice skating with me. She was a cutie in my chemistry class—we had quite the chemistry, you could say . . . okay, sorry, bad joke. We were both 16.

I picked her up and we drove to the rink. Once on the ice, we skated so close together that we actually bumped into each other and fell, just like in a movie. But unfortunately, nothing remarkable happened while we were skating; no big signs that she liked me, no big signs that she didn't like me. We went back to her place after and watched a movie. I guess she didn't like me because we didn't go out again. I failed that "chemistry test," didn't I? Sorry, last bad joke.

Several years ago back here in Arizona, I took a girl ice skating as our first date. We both had lots of fun, neither of us fell and got hurt, which is always a plus. But like so many others, it didn't click for me. I believe she was interested at least in going out on another date, but I didn't ask her out again after that.

Creative Date #84

Master Chef

It's Friday night and you're going out for a flavorful, delicious, expertly prepared dinner. Mmmm, yummy. But there's a twist: you'll be the one cooking that dinner. Say what?

Grab your date and sign up for a cooking class. Cooking classes are a great way to learn some new culinary skills while doing something different for a date. There is sure to be good interaction with your partner as you learn from a professional chef how to cook an amazing meal. Even if you are already a culinary master, chances are your date may not be, so don't let that stop you from trying out this idea. Strap on an apron, put on that chef's hat, and cook something.

What you need for this date:

Check online to find cooking classes near you. The culinary schools sometimes have one-time classes in the evenings when they are not teaching their normal classes during the day.

My commentary on this date:

A few years ago, I decided to attend a cooking class at Sur La Table. There was one 5 minutes away from my work so it was very convenient to go there after my day was over. I would have liked to have brought a date, but at the time couldn't think of anyone that I wanted to take, so I went alone. I was pretty much the only single guy there . . . awkward. But that was okay. There were about 8 other couples there all eager to learn how to make some magnificent food.

The main course we learned how to make was cedar-planked salmon. It was amazing. While taking the class, I couldn't help but notice all the couples there with me. They looked so happy, whether married or not, and like they were genuinely interested in being with each other. I vowed to someday take a date to a cooking class. Then I went to McDonald's and got a cheeseburger. I was still hungry.

Chapter 5: Movie Dates

"Theaters are Out" – A more imaginative way to watch a movie

First off, don't get me wrong, I like going to the movie theaters a lot, but sometimes it is nice to put some thought and effort into it and create a fun and unique place to watch a movie. This next chapter focuses on interesting ways to watch a movie that don't involve the Theater. Trust me—it'll be romance galore.

Creative Date #85

Tents and Movies

Watching a movie at your house or going to the theater gets really old really fast. There are several things that you can do to make watching a movie more creative and romantic. One way is by setting up a tent in your backyard and bringing in your television, Blu-Ray player, or DVD player, as well as pillows and blankets and bean bags. You can make it fun by watching a scary movie, or romantic by watching a chick flick. If you have one of those huge two-room tents you could set up a dinner in one room and have the movie in the other room. Once again, the impressiveness of this date is not really the food that is cooked or lack thereof, or even the movie that you watch, but the time, effort and thought that is put into it.

What you need for this date:

To make this date work you need a tent, a place to set it up (the backyard works well), a really long extension cord, and a TV that will fit in the tent. To make it comfortable you also need things like pillows and blankets. You could even put your sound system in the tent for superior sound quality.

My commentary on this date:

My brother did this for a girl that he'd been dating. He set up our big tent in the back yard, and brought out a TV and VCR (yes, it was the stone age), as well as pillows and beanbags. His girlfriend loved it.

This date is one that's probably best suited for when you know each other well. If it's an early date, at least make sure she's really digging you, or it might just end up being more awkward than fun.

Creative Date #86

Outdoor movie

Ever get tired of doing the same old dinner and a movie date? What if you kept the dinner part, but instead of going to a movie theater, do something really cool and set up a place in your backyard to watch a movie. It is a lot more creative and romantic than the boring seats in the local movie theater. This idea is similar to the watching a movie in the tent, but instead you give it more of an open-air cinema feel.

What you need for this date:

For this date you need a projector and a sound system to hook up to it. If you don't have a nice system, then one of the tabletop mini-systems will work. You also need a screen. If you don't have a retractable screen, like one that you would use for watching a slideshow, then you can always use a white sheet. The portable screen is nice because it has its own stand and you can set it up anywhere. If you use a sheet it will be more difficult to rig, but you can still hang it from a rope in between two trees or from the side of the house. I believe you can even rent one from a store.

Remember, this date takes time and effort to setup, which is what makes it special. Make sure to pick a night when it is not going to rain.

You will also need an extension cord, as well as a power strip. Also, make sure to pick a romantic movie, if that is the genre she likes best. Think of the points you'd score on that one.

My commentary on this date:

My brother used this idea with his wife all the time, before they were married. He borrowed a projector from work and used my dad's portable screen, then set up a sound system to complete it. I think they watched an Indiana Jones movie, not really romantic, but I guess these dates don't always have to be romantic. You can make it more romantic by having it just be you and the girl and a chick flick, but you can also make it a fun group date and watch some other kind of movie.

Sometimes your local city or community will put on outdoor movie events. I know here in the Phoenix area, they usually play Christmas movies in the park. Twice a year, my community has an outdoor movie they set up in a retention basin. They rent this whole inflatable set-up, where the movie screen is actually one big inflatable screen. It's pretty amazing. I have been several times with friends and their spouses . . . yes, I was the fifth wheel, but that is fine. So you could find out when there's a community outdoor movie night if you don't want to set up something yourself.

Creative Date #87

MTV has Nothing on Us!

Making music videos is a ton of fun. Now it has become easier and easier for people to make home videos, wedding videos, corporate videos, music videos—basically any kind of movie you want to make.

Digital video cameras have come way down in price since they were first released, and with smart phone technology the way it is, practically everyone has a video recording device nestled in their pocket. Now after recording, you can hook up the camera to your computer and edit your video or download it from your phone. Most computers have some sort of editing system on them already. For this creative date idea, you and your date can make a music video together. Maybe you could make a lip sync video to one of your favorite love songs or you could make a fun music video, or a silly dancing movie. Holiday seasons are a great time for movie making, so take advantage of whichever one is near.

What you need for this date:

You really only need a camera, whether on your phone or a separate camera, your imagination, and a computer to edit the videos on.

You can find basic editing tutorials on YouTube if you don't really know how to do it already.

My commentary on this date:

My brother and his wife used to make Christmas music videos every year. The videos are really entertaining and fun for the whole family to watch, not to mention it is a great way to save memories for posterity. Something to remember is that this can be a time-consuming task, although that might be what makes it so great! And remember that you don't have to make it a masterpiece; having fun is what really will set this date apart.

Once you're done recording, put it on a DVD or Blu-Ray, keep the file on your computer, or just upload it to YouTube and share it with the world (you'll need to be mindful of copyright issues if you upload to YouTube). And don't fret if it seems like way too much work—the recording and editing can be done over a series of dates. Maybe you could tell your date that for the next few Friday nights you will be working on the video together.

My career is video production so this is something I have lots of experience with. For me sometime in the future maybe I will have my wife be my co-host on my YouTube cooking channel.

Creative Date #88

Movie in a Fort

Want a really fun date that is free? Did you ever make forts when you were a child in your living room or family room? Making forts with chairs and pillows and blankets is really fun. For this activity, you make a fort with your date and then set your TV inside, or build the fort around your TV if it is in an entertainment center. Then make it as comfortable as you want inside with pillows, blankets, love sacs, and cuddle up and watch a movie. If you are going to watch a movie at home, why not make it a little more creative?

What you need for this date:

You don't need anything except what you already have at home. Making a fort is very easy. One of my favorite floor plans is setting up the kitchen table chairs in a large circle, and then putting a big blanket on top. I would put books down or tape the blanket in place. You place sofa cushions on the sides and leave one chair as the crawl space entrance. Then take pillows and blankets inside.

My experience with this date:

When I was a junior in college I met this girl, Kelsey, at the climbing gym where I worked out. She seemed like a nice girl and was pretty cute, too. Plus, she liked climbing, which sealed the deal for me. I suggested that we see a movie sometime because she said she liked them. I picked her up from her house and took her to the Olive Garden. We had a nice dinner and conversation, then went to a movie.

We went back to my condominium where my roommates and some other friends were over. My date had a bit of a headache, but she wasn't quite ready to go home yet, so we gave her some Advil and just relaxed. My roommates decided to make a fort and watch a movie in it. So we barged in on their activity and joined them. During the movie, Kelsey gave me a back massage by driving a toy tractor on my back while I was lying down. Okay, kind of weird, but it felt good. She seemed pretty interested in me. After we watched the movie we played games and decided to stay up all night and then make breakfast in the morning. We made bacon, eggs, and hash browns at around 6:00am, and then I took my date home around 7. I was just going with the flow with this date and she seemed to really enjoy it.

It was actually pretty funny because the fort stayed in our living room for a week. My roommate slept in there, too. College kids.

Creative Date #89

Laptop Movie in the Park

Movies are one of America's favorite pastimes. If you are planning on watching a movie for your date and you want to make it more creative and romantic than just watching one at the theater or at your home, watch it at a park. Set out a blanket and bring a laptop that has a DVD drive, or download a digital copy of it. Bring some popcorn and bottled drinks, and of course bring those treats. Afterwards you could cuddle and enjoy a nice conversation under the stars before returning home.

What you need for this date:

You will need a laptop with an extra battery, blankets to sit on and cuddle with, pillows, any snacks that you want to bring, and a nice place to have the date. This date probably will only work when it is dark outside, otherwise you'll barely be able to see the screen. You might want to use this idea in the summertime, depending on where you live. For example, California would be a great place for it, but where I live in Arizona, not so much.

My commentary on this date:

Several times I have walked around parks near my old college and the only lights I'd see were those of laptop screens, with silhouettes of two people cuddling on a blanket as they watched a movie on it. Too bad I didn't have some water balloons with me. Just kidding—I'm a nice guy, I swear. Laptop movies in the park were a pretty popular creative date activity years ago where I went to school. We need to bring this activity back—bring it to the masses!

Creative Date #90

Driveway Movie

Since movies are a very popular thing to do for a date, I'm sure you've noticed that there are a lot of dates that involve them. This idea is another creative movie date.

Instead of going to a drive-in to watch a movie, which is also really fun, if you can find one these days (they seem to be going extinct), get an extension cord and run it out to your car, set up a TV and DVD/Blu-Ray player, and watch the movie in your driveway. Set out blankets and pillows to make it more comfortable. If you have a really small car then maybe you can set up the TV on a table in front of your car or on the hood, and have external speakers set up inside the car and then sit in your front seats and watch. A cool idea would be to drive to a seaside cliff, or up a mountain, and enjoy the fresh air and spectacular scenery.

What you need for this date:

You will need a TV that will go either inside your vehicle or outside. You will need an extension cord, DVD/Blu-Ray player, and table if the setup is outside. Some cars nowadays come with a DVD player in them and a small screen to view movies on while in the car. If you have one of those then you are set, unless you want a bigger screen. You also can have any snacks and comfort items that you want. Make it funny by rolling out a red carpet that leads to the entrance of the car. This would be better if you had a big cargo van or something like that to watch the movie in.

My commentary on this date:

A long time ago my older brother took the TV and put it in our 1974 Volkswagen Bus. He ran an extension cord from the house out to the van and also brought out a VCR. He took the middle seat out to make it roomier. Then he and his date watched a movie inside. Being the youngster that I was at the time, I just thought he was silly—I mean, there was a perfectly good TV in the family room that wasn't being used. But since I had a habit of pestering him and his dates when they were in the house, it was probably a good idea they were outside in the bus.

Chapter 6: Holiday Dates

"From Christmas to Halloween" – Dates for all occasions

It's time to get your "theme" on. Who doesn't like a nice holiday themed party? From Halloween costume activities to ugly Christmas sweater parties, this last chapter will focus on specific date ideas surrounding various holidays. This chapter will barely scratch the surface of what can be done, so let your imagination run wild.

Creative Date #91

Dinner and a Haunted House

Halloween is a fun time of the year. Some of the finest creativity comes along during Halloween. Not only the costumes that people come up with, but all the fun scary things to participate in such as haunted houses, haunted woods, haunted corn mazes, and costume parties. For a fun group date, get together and make dinner first. The Calzone recipe works really well for this date, or the barbecue pork sandwiches but you can pretty much make whatever you want. After making dinner together and eating, take a ride to the haunted house.

These dates are especially fun because if you are lucky, your date will be hanging on your arm the whole time. She'll be scared out of her mind, but still, it's a win for you and might be your only chance to get close to your date. Just kidding, if you play your cards right, there will be plenty of other chances.

What you need for the date:

This date is quite simple to prepare. All you need are the ingredients for the dinner, or a restaurant to go to. However, I prefer to make dinner with my date, especially in a group setting, because there is a lot of talking and interaction going on. You really get to know your date and the food is good and can be inexpensive.

You should also make sure there would be tickets available for you when you go to the haunted house. If it means getting tickets early, then do it. It might be fun to dress up, as well. The cool thing about these ideas are that they are just ideas; it is up to you how you make it happen. My idea may only be something that triggers your creativity, which leads to an entirely different date.

My experience with this date:

Several years ago in college, I met this really cute girl. She lived in my apartment complex and went to my same college. She was a tall blue-eyed blonde with a fantastic accent from her home state of Georgia. Wow, a killer combination. After chatting with her, I found out that she really likes scary stuff. A light bulb went on in my head and I decided to invite her to a haunted house.

I planned this group date where we made homemade calzones, then drove to a large city about an hour away where the haunted house was located. The drive up was okay, but it seemed like I was the one doing most of the talking. She didn't seem too interested in asking me questions or getting to know me. I brushed that notion aside and decided not to worry about it. When we arrived there was a really long line to get in. We waited patiently and talked within the group. There were a few workers dressed up trying to scare the patrons waiting in line. The Haunted house was amazing, probably one of the best that I have been to. I never really got scared but the make-up and costumes were realistic, and the atmosphere and sound effects added to the already creepy mood. The best part was that this cute girl was on my arm the whole time. It was a really fun date.

On the drive home, it was more of the same, me talking the whole time and her not really responding. Since it was a lot of fun and I liked her I decided to ask her out again. I knew that one of her favorite restaurants was Red Lobster, so we did a double date and went there. Afterwards, since she really likes scary movies, we went and saw the movie, *The Ring*. It was another fun date. Things seemed to me moving the right direction, or were they? Alas, despite my fondness for her, it wasn't meant to be.

Creative Date #92

Halloween and Romance?

This is a good example of a combination of ideas for a date. It can be considered a marathon date because it lasts such a long time. I don't always advise doing a marathon date unless you know for sure it is going well. Sometimes the girl is really nice and will go along for the ride, even though she doesn't really want to be there, which is never an ideal situation. Yeah, dating is tough sometimes. Not that I would know from personal experience or anything . . .

For this activity, pick up your date and take them to a haunted house, or woods, or something else Halloween related. Then go to a scary or romantic movie afterwards—in other words, more cuddle action— and when your date thinks the night is over, pull over at a local park and take a walk, look at the stars, or dance. This works well with a flirty date because there is a lot of physical contact throughout the night. However, your date might just be one of those "overly flirty for their own good" types of people, so be aware. Just because she cuddles with you or holds your hand or your arm doesn't mean she is interested, unless of course your date happens to be your spouse or significant other.

What you need for this date:

Like the other Halloween date, make sure that you will be able to actually get into the haunted place. It never hurts to be prepared. Then have a movie picked out beforehand, which is always better than showing up to the theaters and asking your date what she would like to see. Take some initiative and see what you think you both would like. Next, if you plan to do something after the movie, such as dancing in the park, have a portable music player or speaker with you, and some good songs picked out.

My experience with this date:

One night many moons ago, I was at a dance party and wound up meeting this girl Courtney. I actually knew her in high school but had never really talked to her. We talked and had a good time dancing. I found out that she really liked haunted houses, so I asked her if she wanted to go the next day with me. She said yes. Right away I could tell that she was kinda flirty, so I planned the events for the next night around that knowledge.

First I picked her up in my parents old 1974 Volkswagen Bus. I had another car I could have driven but I knew she loved those old buses. We went to the haunted house and right away there was good physical chemistry. My smile widened every time she hugged me, or squeezed my hand. Afterwards, I took her to the movies, at her request. We saw the movie *For the Love of the Game*. It was an okay movie, and yes, we actually did watch the movie, despite what you are thinking. There was a little cuddle action going on, and I could sense that she wanted me to kiss her, but I didn't. And yes, this is where I can hear you asking why in the world I didn't do it. I guess I wasn't ready to kiss her, or I was too shy to do it.

After the movie, at about 11:00pm, she asked me, "So what are we going to do next?" and I replied with, "I have something up my sleeve." She waited anxiously to see what I had planned. You see, I had planned out what I would do if the date went well, and since the date was definitely going well, I decided to proceed with the next phase of operation "woo her." I pulled the bus over at a local park. I got out and let her out of the car. She was confused, but a big smile came to her face when I turned on the radio that I had brought and asked her to dance. We danced for some time in the park; got a little kissing action in as well. Sounds like a good date, right? Well it was, it was a great date, yet in the end it didn't work out. But I will always remember that night when I impressed even myself with how to woo a girl.

Creative Date #93

Get Yo'self Through That Maze

In October, some places in the United States, and possibly in other countries, make mazes out of the cornfields for some Halloween fun. There are also life-sized hedge mazes that you can visit kind of like the move *The Shining* or even the movie *Labyrinth*. It is pretty fun to go to places like this and try and find your way out. It makes it even more festive if you go when it is dark outside. The Halloween-themed corn mazes usually have people dressed up walking around trying to scare you, too. This would be an excellent idea for a date, either with just the two of you or with a group.

What you need for this date:

You can look online to find the nearest corn or hedge maze to you. The cost is usually very reasonable per person.

My experience with this date:

I have some really good friends that are married who decided to hook me up on a blind date. I am always a bit leery about blind dates because there is so much involved. You don't know if you are going to be attracted to them, if you will click, or have anything in common. A good matchmaker can usually weed out the basics and if he or she knows what you like, they can do a pretty good job, at least with the setup. But the clicking still has to happen.

The plan was that I would show up at my friends' house and my date would be waiting there with my friends since she knew them already. First, we would eat pizza and play games at my friend's house, and then afterwards we would go to a local corn maze. I had heard a little bit about this girl so I was optimistic, and since my friends are pretty good matchmakers I wasn't letting any pessimism about the blind date get the best of me.

After arriving at my buddy's place, I was immediately drawn to the girl. Way cute, gorgeous in fact; I knew I was in trouble. I was quite excited to get to know her. We ate pizza, had a fun time playing games, then we were off to the corn maze. She seemed interested in getting to know me; she asked me questions and laughed when I made jokes. We went on a haunted hayride and walked through the corn maze. It was really fun. There was a big crowd there that night. Some people were dressed up, others were there with families, and there were lots of college students who seemed to be on dates. As the night went on, though, I found out that we really didn't have much in common. I thought she was way cute and it would've been fun to keep going out, but the magic just wasn't there for either of us. Darn.

Creative Date #94

Light up Your Life

There are a lot of fun things to do during Christmas time. One thing that is enjoyed by many is looking at all the decorated houses. There are some pretty spectacular displays that are put on during Christmas. People's homes become mountains of lights and eclectic decorations. There always seems to be one neighborhood nearby that has gone full-blown Clark Griswold.

For another free evening, take your date around to some of the neighborhoods that have amazing lights. It is a pleasant time of year to be out and enjoying the Christmas spirit. Some major cities will have a big tree all lit up downtown, which would be fun to go see. The Phoenix Zoo has an amazing light display in late November thru early January; maybe the zoo closest to you has one, as well. Other light displays that might peak your interest include the LDS Temples located in Salt Lake City, UT, St. George, UT, Mesa, AZ, Oakland, CA, Los Angeles, CA, San Diego, CA, Washington DC, Hamilton, New Zealand, Sydney, Australia, and Manila, Philippines. These locations all put on spectacular lighting displays during the holidays, and usually have Christmas related concerts as well.

What you need for this date:

Transportation and a place to go is all you need for this to work.

My experience with this date:

One Holiday season in college my friends and I came up with a pretty nice group date idea. I needed a date so I asked a girl out that I had met through a friend of mine. Her name was Isabel. She was a very fun and flirty girl. She wanted really badly to see a Christmas show that was going on in the city; I had tickets for it so I decided to ask her. I told her to dress semi-formal.

When I picked her up at her dorm, I was amazed at how elegant she looked. Simply amazing, I looked forward to an evening with a cute girl on my arm. We met up with my friends and their dates and then drove to a place where we could ride a shuttle into the city. After a nice ride downtown, we went and saw the live action Christmas show. The show was like a dance festival, with performers doing dances from their native countries, basically to show how they celebrate Christmas around the world. It was a wonderful spectacle; our eyes were glued to the stage as the dancers performed. Afterwards, we went around and looked at the Christmas lights. Most cities put up some kind of light display downtown. It was really fun. I am not completely sure why I didn't go out with her again, but I tend to think that it was because she didn't return my calls.

I have on occasion taken dates to go look at the amazing light display put on at the Mesa LDS Temple in Arizona; it is one of the most incredible light displays I have ever seen. Another thing that is pretty cool is they also have a 30-minute free Christmas concert pretty much every night in December.

Creative Date #95

Christmas in the Park

Most big cities will have Christmas displays set up downtown. There are usually a lot of fun activities to do there, as well as little temporary shops to browse. Sometimes they even have ice-skating rinks set up.

This might be something nice to do one evening during the holidays. You might be lucky and find a Christmas tree lighting ceremony, run into carolers, find a horse and carriage to ride, or maybe there is an ice sculpting event to attend. Something like this usually won't cost very much money; the biggest expense might be the parking garage.

What you need for this date:

Like a lot of cheap dates, all you need is transportation to the destination. Dress warmly because you will be outside for as long as the date lasts.

My experience with this date:

One year the city had a really nice Christmas set-up downtown near where I lived. There was a special band playing in a tent, there was ice-skating, ice sculptures of the Seven Wonders of the World, and there were little booths set up. I took a girl there. It was a blind date. We looked around at the really cool ice sculptures, and then went inside to listen to the band playing. The music was classical which was very fitting for the setting. My date and I chatted a bit before going back outside to take one more tour of the park and all of its eye candy. It was a pleasant evening, but I really didn't click with the girl, so there wasn't a second date after that. It wasn't a terrible date, though, so definitely something I would do again. I was also on a date one time when I was living in San Jose, California, and we went to downtown San Jose, where there were incredible Christmas displays set up, with vendors, food, and a skating rink. Can we say amazing?

Creative Date #96

It's a Wonderful Life

Start the evening off by making a snowman in the front yard. You could have a snowball fight if you want, wrestle around in the snow, make snow angles, or basically anything that involves fun outside. Of course, this applies to you if you live in a place with snow; if you don't, go for a walk in your neighborhood and look at the lights. Then go inside, make some hot cocoa, pop some popcorn, and watch the movie, *It's A Wonderful Life*. It is a fun and cheap date. Even if you have to rent the movie or buy it, that won't cost you very much. I would get it ahead of time, though, because it is a popular movie, especially around the Holidays.

What you need for this date:

You need snow. If you don't have it, decorate the house together with Christmas decorations or go on that walk I told you about. You need hot cocoa, popcorn, and the movie.

My commentary on this date:

In the process of writing some of the Christmas related dates, I thought to myself, "What do I really like about Christmas?" A few ideas came to me: I like making snowmen, I like hot chocolate, I like popcorn, and I like watching *It's a Wonderful Life*. Then I thought it would make a cool date to combine those. If you don't like the movie choice, choose another Christmas movie to watch, like *Elf*, *The Santa Claus*, or something else Christmas-themed, like one of those sappy Hallmark movies that girls love. Okay, I confess I also like those, and I'm man enough to admit it. But back to the date idea—I find it hard to believe that anyone would not like *It's A Wonderful Life*.

Creative Date #97

Ghost in the Graveyard

For a fun group activity on Halloween, or any other night, go to a nearby cemetery and play a game called "Ghost in the Graveyard."

The game is played like this: Someone is "it" and closes his eyes at the base—which is usually a tree—and counts, "One o'clock, two o'clock, three o'clock . . ." all the way up to 12 o'clock. Then he says, "Ghost in the graveyard, run, run, run," and the other people have to sneak back and try and get to base without getting tagged by the person who is it. It is really, really fun. You could play that or just a normal game of tag at the graveyard, and afterwards sit and tell scary stories. This is a totally free date.

The only thing I'd suggest it that you don't disturb the dead—who knows what might happen . . . queue scary music. Honestly though, if you aren't careful, your game can turn too rowdy, at which time it becomes disrespectful to a place many consider sacred. An alternate option is to play next to the cemetery, or at a park near it.

What you need for this date:

You will need to find a graveyard (cemetery or memorial park) that is open, and then just get your group together and play the game. Or like I mentioned, play next to it, or just in some creepy woods or something.

My commentary on this date:

It was a cool summer evening and I was sitting crouched behind a bush. I could barely peek through the branches and see the creature, my friend, Timmy, patrolling the base. I was breathing heavily. More than once I thought my cover was blown, but staying still kept me hid. Timmy started to run in the other direction; I didn't see who he was after so I made my move. It took only a second to realize he had tricked me; he lured me out perfectly, and now it was a foot race to the base. I took pride in the fact that I was one of the fastest kids in the neighborhood, so knew it shouldn't be a contest. I took long strong strides across the street, and then leaped over a bush; Timmy was getting closer, closer, he slid to tag me, I evaded his move, and tagged base. Wow, that was close.

Many times, I spent evenings with my friends playing this game. We never got bored, never got tired of it. When we got started we only stopped when our mothers called our names. Later in life I had the opportunity to reminisce and play that game again with a big group of friends; the sounds of girls screaming and laughing as they ran to the base or tried to tag someone was pretty cool. Good times. Honestly, the girls that were with us loved this game.

Creative Date #98

Halloween Pumpkin Carving

No matter what your age, a perfect date idea during Halloween for a group or a couple is to carve pumpkins. You can drive to the store together and buy the pumpkins, then take them home, browse the Internet to find the perfect stencil, lie out newspaper on the table and then carve away. You can have a contest to see which group creates the best pumpkin. Make sure to save the seeds, because you can make some fabulous roasted pumpkin seeds. Then after the pumpkins are lit and sitting out on the front porch, go inside, then eat your roasted seeds, make some popcorn, and watch a scary movie.

What you need for this date:

You need to buy the pumpkins and any carving utensils that you will need. The recipe for the roasted pumpkin seeds is below.

Roasted Pumpkin Seeds

Take as many pumpkin seeds as you have and WASH all the slime off them. Pat the pumpkin seeds dry with a paper towel. Preheat the oven to 300. Make sure to sprinkle the seeds with salt; you also can add other seasonings, depending on what you like. You can also coat the seeds with melted butter before you sprinkle them with the seasoning. After that, bake them until golden brown. You will have to stir them once or twice so that they roast evenly.

My commentary on this date:

One chilly October evening, a group of us gathered at a friend's apartment with the idea to have a pumpkin-carving contest. We each were given a pumpkin to carve. An acquaintance of my friend donated 20 of them from her pumpkin patch. I strategically picked one out and while looking at it, came up with a brilliant idea.

When it was time to begin, we all grabbed our carving utensils. I first sketched what I wanted the pumpkin to look like, then after admiring my brilliance, started carving. The other people watched in amazement as my steady hands went about the business of creating a masterpiece. Piece by piece my creation came to life. After about an hour and a half I was finished. Garfield, that witty kitty, sat before me, I impressed even myself that evening. Even though I didn't have a date with me, it was still an amazing evening.

Creative Date #99

Valentine's Day Surprise

Valentine's Day Surprise is a homemade creative dinner. The dinner is made beforehand and served to you and your special someone. Afterwards, you can exchange your Valentine's Day gifts.

It uses elements from other dates that I have already mentioned. The basics of the date are a nice candle light dinner set up in the home, which is made to look like a restaurant. Then fancy menus are laid out in front of you and a friend or relative is there to serve you. This date idea could work nicely with couples who have older kids; you could have them serve you, and while you are eating and dancing, they can be watching a movie in another room. You could even make some homemade dessert for the evening, like homemade peanut butter cups or chocolate covered strawberries. Check out my cooking show on YouTube, *In the Kitchen with Matt,* for some great dessert recipes.

What you need for this date:

The items needed for this type of date are listed for you below in the commentary.

My commentary on this date:

My brother did this for his wife. He gave me this idea and it was really awesome and had some elements of my own creativity, so I decided to include it. In his own words he wrote:

"The "home" restaurant: I just did this for my wife for Valentine's. I couldn't get a reservation at a decent restaurant so I created a fancy restaurant at home. I used our China and fancy wine glasses for the water, cloth napkins, and flowers for a centerpiece and several candles for "atmosphere." I printed a dinner menu using fancy fonts and had everything prepared and ready to serve, or warming in the oven. The restaurant part went like this: I enlisted our 12 ½ year-old daughter to dress up and act as the hostess and our 11 year-old son to dress up and act as the waiter.

When my wife came down from upstairs, dressed for an evening out, I escorted her down the hall to the kitchen and our daughter greeted us as the hostess and seated us at the coffee table I had prepared earlier. We sat on the floor, Japanese style, and then "our hostess" brought us the salads I had prepared in advance. Our son introduced himself as our waiter and brought sourdough rolls and real butter (restaurants always use real butter) to go with our salads. When our salads were finished, our plates were cleared and the dinner was served (already prepared and warming in the oven). We ate and talked and with the food being served and taken care of, it really was like being in a restaurant. Since it was Valentine's, we exchanged cards and gifts and had a great time.

We then went out to hit a movie, but the highlight was definitely the dinner "in." Our son and daughter were great as hostess and waiter. Roommates/friends can be used as waiter/host if no children are old enough to help or if you don't have any children. The whole thing cost less than $45 but would have cost double that in a restaurant, and been much less memorable. I do recommend that before this is done, make sure you know how to cook the food. Fancy food like seafood and steaks work great for the home restaurant, but for the first timer, it would be a bad time to experiment and over/under cook something for a big date."

Creative Date #100

Halloween Costume Theme

Have you ever been to a Halloween party and seen couples matching some cool theme? That is what this date is all about. Go shopping together to the Halloween store, costume shop, or wherever else and pick some matching costumes. You could go as Ghostbusters, Blues Brothers, Star Wars characters, cartoon characters, or maybe dress up like a famous couple from the current era or eras past. The possibilities are endless. Make sure to be dressed up for whatever place you plan to eat at before going to your party. Even if it isn't a party and you are only dressing up to take the kids out trick-or-treating, it will still be a lot of fun. There are plenty of Halloween-themed dances that you can attend as a "matching" couple, as well.

What you need for this date:

You only need the materials for the costumes. You can get cheap costume components at a place like Goodwill or Salvation Army, or if you are handy with a needle and thread, fabric stores usually have good prices. For the sewing impaired, you can rent or buy costumes at a costume shop.

My commentary on this date:

One Halloween, years ago, my friend and I dressed up and went to a Halloween party. The usual costumes were present, but the hit of the night was when my brother and his fiancée showed up. My brother was dressed as a devil. The make-up was amazing. We'd had plenty of costume make-up practice because we made a movie years ago, which featured many monsters. My brother said it took about three hours or so to get his face to look like the devil. His fiancée was dressed as an angel. They made a perfect couple. I have been to many Halloween parties and dances since then, and each were a fun night. Most recently, I went to a Halloween-themed country-dancing event, which was such a great experience.

Creative Date #101

Let There Be Fireworks

One of the greatest and ancient of manmade spectacles is a fireworks display. Fireworks were invented in China in the 7th century. Originally, the reason was to scare away evil spirits, but as time has gone on they have now become part of many cultures to celebrate various holidays or other events and religious celebrations. You'll be able see fireworks shows almost anywhere worldwide on New Year's Eve, and here in the United States, you can find multiple displays over the 4th of July. Disneyland puts on some amazing fireworks shows as well, and you don't have to wait for a holiday to see those.

Whatever the occasion, grab a date, turn your face to the night sky, and maybe even cuddle up on a blanket. Be amazed as little bits of combustible paper tubes are shot up like rockets into the air and explode, showering the sky with wondrous colors. Who knows, maybe you will take that opportunity to make your own "fireworks" with your date.

What you need for this date:

This date idea is fairly straightforward; look online for a cool fireworks display to attend. Then, depending on the venue, you may or may not need to bring a blanket and chairs. Maybe bring some snacks and drinks to enjoy before and after the display. Again, it will depend on the type of venue that you attend.

My experience with this date:

I have attended fireworks displays on numerous occasions. I have always been fascinated with fire and fireworks, and was even a bit of a pyro in my younger years. One evening sticks out in my mind. Several years ago while in college, my roommates and I took our dates out to dinner and then drove over to a large golf course that was going to be putting on a fireworks display for the 4th of July. We put out blankets and talked until the show began. It was an amazing show set to some classic rock music. I will never forget the finale set to Neil Diamond's "America". Probably the best fireworks show I have ever seen. On another occasion I was with a buddy of mine and we were attending a concert on one of the piers in San Francisco. Afterwards, they had an amazing fireworks display shooting out over the bay which was simply incredible.

Chapter 7: Gift Ideas

"Something Other than Chocolates"

Need a few gift ideas other than the cliché flowers and chocolates for your date? This bonus chapter will include a handful of creative gift ideas that are sure to impress. Don't get me wrong, picking up roses from the store and buying a box of chocolates is still a fine idea, but you can certainly kick up the creativity once in a while.

Creative Idea #1

"I Wanna Hold Your Hand"

Since the beginning of MTV in the 80's, people have enjoyed watching their favorite stars playing their favorite music first on television, and now on media like YouTube. A creative idea is to make your own music video, which is by far one of the coolest things that you can do. Remember the date idea where you made one together? Well now you get to make one by yourself as a gift for that special someone.

You really have to know the person well and have been dating or already married before you do something as grand as making a lip sync music video for them. This is where we separate the men from the boys (and women from the girls) when it comes to creativity. You can put the video onto a DVD/Blu-Ray or just give them the video file and then they can watch it over and over again.

What you need for this idea:

You need some sort of video camera, whether its own device or on a phone. To edit the video you need a computer. Most computers come with some sort of editing software. The one I prefer is Adobe Premiere. This a professional editing software, so most likely something cheaper will suffice for your needs. If you have Windows, the chances are good that your computer came with something like Microsoft Movie Maker, which is very basic software, but will work fine. You'll also need to bring a portable radio with you or an iPod, or just your phone, as long as it's not also your camera. It is very important that you rehearse the song over and over, so that your lips match up well with the words, otherwise it looks really funny. Then you go out with a friend and film yourself lip singing with the song. I usually film it in many different locations so that I can edit them together.

My commentary on this idea:

On two occasions growing up, my older brother made a music video for his girlfriend. The first one was his high school girlfriend. The second was for his wife. Some songs he made videos of include: "Ice Cream Man" by Van Halen, "Girl You Know It's True" by Milli Vanilli (yeah, this dates my brother), "I Wanna Hold Your Hand" by The Beatles, and many other songs. He did a Chicago song, too. I have yet to make a music video for a girl that I like, because this sort of thing would probably creep a girl out unless you'd been dating awhile.

While still in college in Utah, I helped my buddy make a lip sync music video for his wife for Valentine's Day. I planned out the whole thing for my friend because he didn't have too much experience with this sort of thing. The song was examined and locations written down for each set of lyrics. Then we drove around and filmed at those locations. I edited the video, which took a pretty long time, then put it on a DVD for my buddy. He got his wife flowers and then gave her the present. She absolutely adored the video.

Creative Idea #2

Neighborhood Bouquet

If you want to bring your date flowers maybe you can do something like this to make it extra special. I got the idea from the movie *Phenomenon*. In it, John Travolta is on his way to the house of the girl that he likes; he stops along the way and picks different species of flowers on the way from his house to hers. All the different flowers made a really spectacular bouquet.

You don't have to spend tons of money on flowers when you can pick them locally. Granted, there may not be a lot of flowers growing in your area, and you shouldn't go stealing your neighbors' flowers, but I am willing to bet if you ask people if you could pick just one flower, and that it was for a good cause, you could put together a pretty nice homemade bouquet.

What you need for this idea:

You need flowers, and something nice to tie them together, like a ribbon. It would be nice if the flowers happened to be her favorite or at least some of her favorite colors. Make the ribbon her favorite color, at the very least.

My experience with this idea:

I wanted to bring my date flowers one time many years ago, so instead of going to the store, I walked into my backyard and picked them. I got permission from my mom first, because there is no telling how mad people will get if you go rogue and snip away at someone's garden uninvited. As for my mom, she wants me to get married, so there wasn't a problem when it came to clipping flowers. She even helped me trim them so they looked all nice and perfect, then found a ribbon for me to use. Ah, isn't that sweet? My date really liked them.

Creative Idea #3

Write a Poem

Writing a poem is definitely not an easy task, and sometimes it might be cheesy, but it works. People love getting things that were made or written especially for them. If you want to tell your significant other how you feel in a way other than the ordinary or customary, you could write a poem for them. The poem doesn't have to be some masterful work of literary genius, but can be simple and sweet. To get ideas you can check out a poetry book from the library, or find a how-to article or video online to help you write it. A poem would make a wonderful present for a birthday or Valentine's Day, and it also would make a really good "just because" present. It could be one of those little notes that you attach to the outside of their car, or put in an envelope and drop in their mailbox.

What you need for this idea:

You need your brain, your inspiration, and a pen or computer. You could write the poem and then add clip art or other pictures to it and laminate it or frame it, or just fold it up. An interesting idea would be to put it in a nice envelope, then wrap some red ribbon around it with a rose attached. Have it sitting on her dinner plate. You could use one of the romantic dinner date ideas that I have written about or come up with one of your own.

My commentary on this idea:

I have written poems before. Just not for anyone special yet. I have a friend who wrote one for his wife for her birthday. She loved it, and the poem was so good that she sent it to a publisher, and it got published.

The Look in Your Eyes

A poem by *Matt Taylor*

I can't help but notice

The look in your eyes

Magical, incredible, leaves me hypnotized.

I can't help but notice

The way you touch me,

Amazing, wonderful, incredible glee.

I can't help but notice

The beauty of your face

Gorgeous, lovely, full of grace.

I can't help but notice

The way that we'll be,

Charming, fascinating, the way you love me.

I just wrote this poem while writing this section. It took me about fifteen minutes. I didn't even have a girl in mind, as I was writing it; I guess I was thinking about how I would want to feel when I looked into my future significant other's eyes.

Creative Idea #4

Fortune Cookie Surprise

This idea isn't a whole date itself, but can be accompanied with a many of the dates outlined in this book. First, you type up your own fortune and place it in a fortune cookie. You can buy these at various stores or you can make your own. If you don't have a recipe for fortune cookies in your favorite recipe book, just look one up online—you'll find plenty of recipes. After you have your cookie and the special note inside, slyly give it to the waiter and have it delivered at the end of the dinner. This is not my personal idea, but it is one that I have heard about a lot, and have seen in various movies/TV shows, and couldn't help but include it.

What you need for this idea:

You don't need much and the little expense that it takes will be worth it. Just type up the fortune on a typewriter or on your computer and print it out and put it in the cookie. The delivery of the cookie might be tricky, but that is part of the fun and creativity of the idea.

My commentary on this idea:

This probably isn't something you would do early on in a relationship, although it can be done as a joke, to get your date to laugh, or for some other fun occasion. I have heard of people doing this for proposals, which would be great. It can be romantic or silly, it is up to you.

Some Last Thoughts

I have enjoyed writing this book and sharing some of my creativity with you all, as well sharing my experiences that I have had with these ideas. I am very grateful for the support that I have received from my friends and family while writing this book. And of course, a special thanks to my editor, for all the hard work she put into editing this book.

I hope this book will give you a great starting point for making your dates a bit more creative. I should also mention that I don't think that every one of your dates needs to be some creative feat of excellence, but I am sure your date, spouse, girlfriend, or boyfriend, will appreciate something well thought out once in a while. I am curious as to how these dates work out for you. Thanks again for reading my book.

Resources

A website with castles (from Sunday Drive Date, Date #5)

    http://www.dupontcastle.com/castles/

A website with ghost towns (from Ghost Town Date, Date #13)

    http://www.ghosttowns.com

Websites with cave listings (from Caving Adventure Date, Date #66)

    http://cavern.com/

    http://www.showcaves.com/english/usa/caves/

Website for geo-caching (from Geo-caching, Date #78)

    http://www.geocaching.com

Author's YouTube Cooking Channel

    https://www.youtube.com/user/inthekitchenwithmatt

Made in the USA
Columbia, SC
15 December 2020